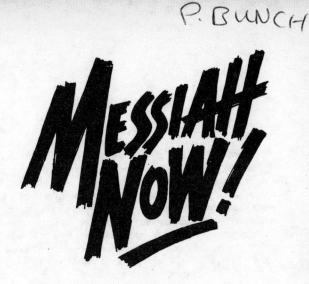

# MESSIAH NOW!

## David Zeidan

Ten true stories from modern-day Israel
of men and women who met Yeshua

Foreword by Helen Shapiro

OM Publishing
Carlisle, England

Scripture quotations are taken from the New International
Version, © 1973, 1978, 1984 by International Bible Society and
published in Britain by Hodder and Stoughton Ltd.

**British Library Cataloguing-in-Publication Data.**

A catalogue record for this book
is available from the British Library.

ISBN 1-85078-115-X

OM Publishing is an imprint of
Send The Light (Operation Mobilisation),
PO Box 300, Carlisle, Cumbria, CA3 0QS, England.

Production and printing in England by
Nuprint Ltd, Station Road, Harpenden, Herts., AL5 4SE.

# Contents

Foreword by Helen Shapiro 9
Introduction 11

1. Yossi—Not Seeking Yet He Found! 13
2. Shira—A Kibbutz Girl Finds the Messiah 29
3. Israel Segal—An Officer Finds Peace 47
4. Maja—From Atheism to Faith 65
5. Shaul—Dreams and Visions 73
6. Tali—Yearning for Meaning 85
7. Yaakov—A Marine Finds the Way 95
8. Batyah—Typesetting a Strange Book 107
9. Israel Harel—From Death to Life 117
10. Hadassah—Through Crisis to Faith 133

Postscript 153
Glossary 155

# Acknowledgements

*I am very grateful* to my good friend Johan Schep who used his holiday to travel to Israel and to interview the people whose stories appear in this book. Many of them are his personal friends, and this book could not have been written without his help. For that help I express my sincere thanks.

# Dedication

*This book is dedicated* to all my friends in Israel whose stories do not appear in it—although they could have done! The choice was difficult, and I have tried to represent as wide a spectrum as possible. There is no doubt that there are many other stories worth telling amongst the growing number of Israelis known as messianic Jews.

# Foreword

*It is with great joy* that I write the foreword to this book, having read and been inspired by the stories of these ten Israeli Jews, one of whom I know personally.

These Jewish people, whether born in Israel or living there from a very young age, come from quite varied diaspora backgrounds; some from Eastern Europe or Germany, having lost family in the holocaust, others from elsewhere in the Middle East. God brought them into the land for the specific purpose of revealing his truth as part of his great plan in these End Times.

As Israelis they each had to do their military service; then some of them travelled abroad while others stayed on at the kibbutz or town where they came from. Each one came to know Yeshua (Jesus) as Messiah in his or her own way. But the thing which seems to bind them together is that they had to discover the Jewishness of Yeshua and the Brit Hadashah (New Testament) before going on to discover and accept him as the Messiah.

They had to find out, as I did, that Yeshua is not some alien god who isn't meant for the Jewish people; that he's not an enemy who hates us, but that in fact he is the one who came as our brother in the flesh; who was spoken of, prophesied about and promised to the Jewish people in the

Tenach (Old Testament). He is the one who came, as he said, 'to the lost sheep of Israel' and who gave himself as the perfect, atoning sacrifice for our sins. He is the Messiah of Israel, the Son of the Living God, the Saviour of the world.

My own path was through reading the messianic prophecies in the Tenach. I had never read them before. I didn't even know they existed. Jesus had always been presented to me through various media in a way I couldn't relate to with my Hebraic mindset. But having read the prophecies and subsequently the Brit Hadashah for the first time (with some trepidation), it became clear to me that the concept I'd had of him all those years was way off beam. I realised that this New Testament was a Jewish book—not full of anti-Semitism as I'd been led to believe—but a book written by Jews about their Messiah. This comes as a revelation to most of us when we read it for the first time. It certainly did for the people whose stories are in this book.

God is doing a wonderful thing among his people in the land of Israel in these Last Days. In a way not witnessed since the first century CE he is revealing himself to his ancient people. It is marvellous to see the growth of messianic congregations in Israel and around the world and to see Israeli and diaspora Jews coming to know Yeshua in such numbers and in such dramatic and miraculous ways, as he reveals himself to them.

The stories in this hugely enjoyable book are just part of this amazing move of God. They have been compiled so that many, both Jew and Gentile, may be inspired to seek God, who himself says we will find him when we seek him with all our hearts.

Having read these stories, may those truly seeking God read the Scriptures and find out for themselves who Yeshua really is. Amen.

*Helen Shapiro*

# Introduction

*For many years* I had a burden on my heart to see a book published which would tell the interesting stories of Israelis belonging to the messianic movement. I was too busy to do the job myself. However, as no one else undertook this assignment, I finally decided to use a change in my work to edit the life stories of the people appearing in this book. These are all true stories taken from contemporary Israeli society. Most characters appear with their true names, although here and there I have changed the names of secondary characters to protect them from undue exposure.

This book describes a true and little-known chapter of Israeli life. Many will be able to identify with the characters and their life stories. My hope is that this book will contribute to the better understanding of this small but growing sector of the Israeli scene, and that it will also contribute to a greater degree of tolerance and understanding between the many colourful subgroups of Israeli society today.

*David Zeidan*

# 1

# Yossi—Not Seeking, Yet He Found!

*At the age of* sixteen I decided to remove the 'kippah' from my head. Enough of hypocrisy and pretence! I was now old enough to be independent of my parents' customs and traditions, and to follow in the footsteps of my two older brothers who had done the same thing several years back and now led secular lives. I wanted to be like my classmates who enjoyed life without any inhibitions. Parties, smoking, drinking—I wanted to experience it all.

As for God, if he existed, he might once upon a time have created the universe, but he certainly wasn't around any more to intervene, or to control what was happening down here now.

My father wasn't shocked when he saw me without the kippah. He had known all along that it would come to this. He had been through it all before with my two brothers. In fact, he was the main culprit in our rebellion against religion and tradition.

I was born in Haifa in 1960. My parents, both from a religious background, had emigrated to Israel from Turkey.

My father was very involved in the Jewish orthodox way of life, as an official circumciser, kashrut supervisor and teacher preparing boys for their Bar Mitzvah ceremony.

At home we observed all the orthodox traditions. We kept the Sabbath and celebrated the feasts with their specific customs and foods—matzot for Pessach, candles at Hanukkah. We kept the strict laws of kashrut—we did it all. Every Jewish feast was an opportunity for a celebration, yet even as a child I felt that something was lacking.

For my father religion was merely a source of employment and income—and nothing more. To the outside world he acted as a tradition-keeping Jew in every detail, but at home he did only what was convenient to him and acted like any secular Israeli.

This hypocrisy offended my childish sensitivity. Keeping up traditions seemed to be our highest priority but there was hardly any mention of God, who seemed unimportant and delegated to the sidelines. It all lacked spiritual reality and meaning for me.

I was sent first to a religious kindergarten and then transferred to the 'Alliance' secular school in Haifa. At school I met friends who seemed to live in a completely different world from mine—secular and seemingly free. I was also involved in the 'Bnei Akiva' youth movement run by the National-Religious Party where I noticed the same double standards as at home. So as I grew up I gradually arrived at the decision to become secular myself at a suitable age.

At home we had reasonably good relationships with each other. I was always close to my mum, who protected me and supplied me with pocket money and later with cigarettes. She took care of me and I felt free to share my feelings with her. I also had a very good relationship with my brothers. We were good friends and I learnt a lot from them and tried to emulate them to some extent.

With dad things were different. We didn't have any explosive confrontations but our relationship was cool. He was a hard man. I would often lend him a hand in his work and carry heavy loads for him as he had to be careful because of his health—but we were never close to each other.

At school I was a quiet and diligent pupil excelling in mathematics. But that ended in the tenth grade when I took off my kippah. I started to smoke and went out drinking with my friends. My work deteriorated as I neglected my studies. At the end of that term my grades were so low that I was officially warned that unless I improved I would have to leave that school.

I improved sufficiently to continue my studies and to graduate from high school. I remember in the twelfth grade—our final year—some of us stole a key to the school front door. Before exams we would sneak in at night and steal the question papers. We would then revise for these questions and obtain high grades.

I have always loved reading and was a real bookworm. I used to take lots of books from the library, but often 'forgot' to return them.

I was brought up to love our land and nation. I loved Israel's wildlife and landscapes and travelled around a lot enjoying our beautiful countryside. This love for the land is still present with me today. I also wanted to serve my country and give it my very best. My childhood dream was to be a combat pilot. My eldest brother was a flight navigator and I envied him. Later, when I realised that because of my poor eyesight and need to wear glasses I couldn't become a pilot, I was deeply disappointed.

Soon after leaving high school I was called up for military service. I had decided to join an elite combat unit where I could contribute most to the state. I applied for the paratroopers, but the examining psychologist turned me down. My next choice was the Golani brigade, but they had their full quota of recruits and did not need me. My third option was the mobile infantry, who accepted me gladly.

I soon discovered that army life was no joke. Boot camp was in the desert, and we experienced terrible heat, freezing nights and sand storms. We got very little sleep at night and were on the go the whole time. We went on long forced marches with all our gear and officers who seemed bent on aggravating and humiliating us. Discipline was tough—this was the norm for combat units. Their goal was to break us and then recreate us in the military mould.

There were times when things got so tough physically and mentally that I was on the verge of a breakdown, but I did make it!

Actually I learned a lot in the army. I learned that my puny body could do a lot more than I ever imagined to be possible. I learned that will power, coupled with determination, goal orientation and a lot of effort can achieve anything. As we say in Hebrew, nothing can stand up to the will. I also learned to cultivate and enjoy the company of those around me as we lived at close quarters to each other. I have no doubt that the service helped form my character and prepare me for life. Towards the end of my service I was able to fulfil a cherished dream and took part in a parachuting course.

On being discharged, I planned to travel abroad and see the world, feeling that my small and limited society in Israel was getting too stuffy and I needed some fresh air. I did have friends, but no deep relationships. I hoped that abroad I would meet different types of people and be able to forge some personal relationships which would be more meaningful.

On my return home I planned to study computers, set up my own business, make money and be a success in life. These were my dreams. I was however disappointed because the army would not give me a permit to go abroad. The war in Lebanon was about to start, and I was soon recalled to active service.

I was assigned to a tank-hunting unit and we drove north in armoured vehicles. Near the town of Kiryat Shmona our vehicle broke down. Whilst the others drove on we had to stay and wait for the maintenance people to arrive and change our engine. When this was finally done we spent the remaining days of the war chasing after our unit in Lebanon. We eventually caught up with them two hours after the cease-fire! They had succeeded in destroying sixty Syrian tanks without our help.

Since then I do regular reserve duty each year. We often serve in the territories. As I have been through an army medic course I often have to attend to the wounded, both soldiers and Palestinians. I don't hate Arabs; it's a pity they are our enemies and won't accept our right to exist in this land. I am committed to the security of our state but at the same time I try to love the enemy and to treat them as human beings.

After the war I tried again to travel abroad, but the army wouldn't give me a permit for more than two weeks. So I finally decided to travel around Israel instead and enjoy our beautiful country. I took a backpack and a sleeping bag and set off to explore the length and breadth of our little land. My first stop was at the Lake of Galilee. On the beach there I met a young English girl, Henny. I was immediately

attracted to her at that first meeting because there was
something different about her. As we talked I discovered
that she had a deep love for Israel and for the Jewish
people. Somewhat strange for a Gentile, I thought. 'It is
from God,' she told me. 'Yeshua put this special love into
my heart. After all he was a Jew.'

She had this special relationship with God, very direct
and personal. She would talk to him freely as to a friend.
She claimed that he gave her guidance and direction. It all
seemed very strange to me. I decided she had a powerful
imagination and that she assumed her subconscious wishes
were God's will.

Henny was really very nice. I was glad that she enjoyed
my company and was willing to continue her travels with
me. We spent a great week together travelling around the
country, and I was sad to see her fly home to England.

We corresponded and in her letters she again told me
about Yeshua, who she claimed was the Messiah of Israel
and who had given her this love for Israel. God also continued to guide her in the small details of her life.

Around that time I discovered that my mum had been
given a New Testament by some young ladies who had
knocked on our door. I tried reading it but found the
ancient Hebrew too difficult to understand and I fell asleep
whilst trying.

My curiosity was now aroused. Who is this Yeshua? I
wanted to know more about him. I had heard negative
comments about 'Yeshu' as the Rabbis called him. Was it
the same person? Who was he? What did he do and teach?
Why did the Rabbis give him that derogatory name?

Whilst visiting a friend from army days I discovered that
he too had met an English girl with a faith similar to
Henny's. In England one of her friends had forced into his
hands a booklet in Hebrew that he now gladly passed on to

me. It was called *Living Waters* and was actually a Gospel of Matthew in modern, easy Hebrew. I was delighted! This was just for me. As I read through the booklet I came to know something of Yeshua and his life and teaching for the first time in my life.

As a medic I worked for some time in the Rambam hospital in Haifa. Working in the same department were Mary, an Arabic girl and her English friend. As I listened to them chatting amongst themselves I was reminded of Henny.

'Mary,' I said to her one day, 'you remind me very much of my English girl friend Henny. She spoke of her faith in Yeshua exactly as you do.'

'Great,' said Mary, 'why don't you come and visit our congregation? You'll meet many there who believe like her. Jews, Arabs and others.'

I accepted her invitation and visited Bethesda congregation in Haifa. It was during the Purim holiday, and the message was about the book of Esther. They connected it all with the New Testament and Yeshua—I was quite impressed. After the service the young people met for their own activities. During that time someone prayed, and I was struck by his direct and personal relationship with God. His prayer was sincere, powerful and full of feeling—it made a great impact on me. This man wasn't talking to a brick wall, but to someone who was there, alive and listening.

This style of prayer was very different to the prayers I was accustomed to hearing in my childhood. I was used to the formal prayers out of the Siddur—the Jewish prayer book—three times a day. The same words in difficult Hebrew and unintelligible Aramaic would be recited in a mechanical way, repeated so often as a formula that they had lost their meaning. I have no doubt that there are religious people who recite them with great sincerity, but the prevalent attitude would be that summed up by Isaiah:

'These people come near to me with their mouth and honour me with their lips but their hearts are far from me. Their worship of me is made up only of rules taught by men.'

Here was something different. I heard a note of personal faith and relationship with God which I had never experienced before.

I attended that congregation several times, and got to know the people there—Ruth, Mary's friend and flatmate who was an immigrant from the US, Hanan, a successful engineer and his family, Yohanan and many others. They all believed in Yeshua and often spoke about him.

Finally the army gave me a permit to travel abroad and I flew to England. Henny met me at the airport and took me to her home, which became the base for my travels around Britain. I was delighted to see her again and was once more impressed by her sincere faith. I soon realised that all her family had the same faith. Whilst living at her home I was always amongst believers and heard many testimonies of how they came to believe in Yeshua. I was especially impressed by the conversations they had amongst themselves in which God was central. 'Listen to what God did for me today, how he answered my prayers!' 'Would you please pray for me about this matter...' they would say to each other.

I hadn't come across such a personal and intimate relationship with God even amongst orthodox Jews. I noticed that in orthodox Judaism God wasn't as near to us as he was to these believers. Their faces seemed aglow with joy and serenity. There was a wonderful atmosphere in their home, an atmosphere of love that was expressed in words and in actions. I envied them because this was something I had missed in my own family.

I met some of Henny's friends and sometimes attended

their congregation. I felt attracted to their faith but hesitated. 'This isn't for you, Yossi,' I said to myself. 'You are Israeli, Jewish, secular. You don't even believe in God. Why don't you just forget all this nonsense?'

I didn't need God. The army had taught me to trust in myself, in my will power, in my hidden potential. No, I didn't need God, I could get on quite nicely without him. Yet, on the other hand I did wonder about the question of God's existence. Maybe he was there after all! I spent a lot of time thinking about this problem.

I was talking to Henny one day on this subject when she said: 'Why don't you turn directly to God and ask him to give you a sign as a proof that he exists?' It seemed a logical proposition. I immediately turned to him and asked him to do something special for me if he really did exist. I did not ask for money or for material things. I just wanted a clear sign of his existence. I always used to wake up between seven and eight o'clock in the morning without fail. There was no exception, it was like clockwork. 'If you are there, please wake me up at eleven o'clock instead!' I prayed. I repeated this prayer a few times but nothing happened. 'If there's no sign, then there's no God!' I said to myself.

During my sixth week in England I met a believing young fellow under somewhat strange circumstances and I sat up late into the night chatting to him. 'God won't prove his existence to you.' he said. 'He wants you to take a step of faith towards him.' I didn't agree with him, but his words started a fierce struggle within me. 'Yossi, leave all this nonsense, pack up your belongings and get away fast,' said one voice. 'No, wait a moment, you have found something here even if you weren't looking for it,' said another voice within me, 'This is what your heart really desires and it is good for you.'

I remembered the many seemingly random occurrences

that had brought me up to this point in my life and I made a list of them—it was quite long! I suddenly realised that there must be some hidden meaning in all of this that I had never seen before.

Some days later I sat in my room with a New Testament in front of me. 'If you really exist,' I said to God, 'then make me open this book at the passage that you want me to read.' I opened the book at random and my eyes fell on the heading: 'The request for a sign.' It was in Luke's Gospel, chapter 11. Yeshua says to those seeking for a sign at that time: 'This is a wicked generation. It asks for a miraculous sign, but none will be given it except the sign of Jonah.' I was stunned! I understood what Yeshua was saying to the people who were testing him, and I concluded that he was speaking to me and showing me that I shouldn't ask for a sign—yet this was a sign in itself. He had granted my request and it was now up to me to take a step of faith towards him. However, I put off the decision again and again. I wouldn't surrender that easily.

That weekend we attended a concert of a well-known Christian singer, Don Francisco. There was a great crowd of thousands listening to him. The singing was great, there was a wonderful atmosphere and I was deeply moved. At the end of the performance he asked anyone in the audience who wanted to take a step towards God to lift their hand. Many did, but I couldn't. Something seemed to stop me even though later I was sorry I hadn't responded.

Another evening we attended a messianic Jewish congregation in Finchley. The sermon was about Gideon and the fleece of wool—a story from the book of Judges in the Tenach. I felt strangely burdened and knew it was time to decide. I mustn't put it off any longer—but I did.

On the way back on the underground I was attacked by a group of skinheads for no apparent reason. Fortunately for me some plain-clothes detectives appeared on the scene, separated us and arrested some of them. I was dazed. I felt myself all over for damage. My ribs hurt, I had some bruises and a screw on my spectacles had been broken, but otherwise I was unharmed. I was grateful but confused. Why had they attacked me without any provocation? What could it mean? I realised that God had saved my life in a miraculous way that evening.

'What are you waiting for? Why don't you start believing in God?' asked Henny on the way home after the attack.

'Henny,' I said, 'I am not yet totally convinced, though I am almost there.' 'Then ask God to enter your life and help you both to believe and to understand,' she suggested. 'OK,' I answered, 'I'm willing to try that.'

No sooner said then done! That evening in April 1983 I asked Yeshua to come into my life, to forgive my sins and to help me to believe in him.

This was a leap in the dark, a dive into deep waters, a step from which there was no return. I took a step towards him and he came towards me. I opened the door and he entered my life.

From that evening onwards there was a change in me. There were still lots of things I didn't understand, but I now knew that God existed, that Yeshua was the Messiah who had died for my sins and forgiven me and that I now believed in him.

I also became more patient and tolerant and loving towards others. I started studying the Bible with Henny's help and I began to understand why Yeshua had to die as the sacrifice for my sins. He was my substitute. Only through him can I have a personal relationship with God.

I now regularly attended Henny's congregation. One evening they asked anyone who wanted to receive Yeshua to step forward. This time I did not hesitate. I stepped forward and prayed again for Yeshua to enter into my life. I know it wasn't necessary to do it twice, but I wanted to publicly declare my new-found faith.

During those early days of my faith I also felt that God wanted me to give up smoking. I had often tried to quit smoking in the past, but it had always only lasted for a few weeks at a time. This time I threw away the cigarettes knowing it would be for good, and I haven't touched one since. I felt happy and fulfilled as never before.

Three weeks after I came to faith in Yeshua I returned home to Israel. Henny accompanied me. Our relationship had progressed and we planned to get married. Returning home to my parent's flat in Haifa I was faced with the problem of how to introduce my new faith to my parents and friends. At first I spoke to them about Henny and her faith. 'This is what she believes...', I would tell them. Alone in my room I would read the Bible and pray. I was worried lest my mother should come in and see me. What would she think? I had never acted like this before. I felt that I must tell her about it no matter what.

One night as we sat and chatted past midnight I mustered my courage and told her the whole story. I felt a tremendous sense of relief as though a heavy stone had been lifted off my heart. Mum didn't seem too disturbed, her mother's love seemed to cover her son's strange new beliefs.

Having spoken to Mum it was easier to share with my brothers. One of them said: 'Yossi, what shall I say? You should go to a Yeshiva and get to know Judaism better before deciding what you prefer.' Later he said: 'Actually I prefer you as you are now rather than if you became ultra-orthodox. I like you better this way.'

Father was a different kettle of fish. I waited for a month before I felt bold enough to approach him. His response was one of anger and he wouldn't talk to me after that. A fortnight later I tried again. 'Why won't you talk to me?' I asked. 'Because you want to marry a Gentile girl and because you actually believe in that man,' he said. 'I won't talk to you ever again.'

He even threatened to throw me out of the house, but Mum wouldn't let him. He didn't talk to me for a whole year. During that period various friends dropped me after hearing of my faith. That was a price I had to pay as a disciple of Yeshua, but God gave me other friends, brothers and sisters in the faith who filled the void left in my life.

I began a course of studies in architectural engineering and also became involved with the messianic students union. My life was busy and full of meaning and I had a goal—to serve God and to tell others about Yeshua.

A year later on returning home from a stint of reserve duty in the army I found a note from Dad: 'Yossi, take all your books about Yeshua and throw them out of the house.' I wrote him a letter in answer to this note and told him that I was prepared to remove all my books except my New Testament and one other book I was studying at the time. That letter marked a change in our relationship, and he started talking to me again.

For a year and a half he was friendly and then he underwent another drastic change. When he realised that I wouldn't give up my faith he decided to punish me again with his angry silence. He wouldn't even say 'Hello'. We would sit down to a meal at the same table and he would totally ignore me. It was embarrassing and the worst was when I phoned home from reserve duty. If Dad happened to lift the receiver he wouldn't say a word. He would either slam it down or call Mum. That really hurt.

My relationship with Henny did not lead to marriage.

After a time of soul-searching we decided that we were not destined for each other and that it would be better to break off our contact. Henny returned home to England.

Some time later I met Ronit, an Israeli girl from Kibbutz Amiad who also believed in Yeshua. As we got to know each other better our relationship developed and we finally decided to get married. I told Mum that I would like to bring Ronit home for a visit so she could get to know the family and also receive Dad's blessing on our union. Mum passed the message on to him and he was surprised. Why should I want to include him? I explained, again through Mum's good offices, that I respected him as my father and wanted him to get to know Ronit and to give us his agreement and blessing.

Dad was touched and agreed. Ronit came for a visit and Dad was very impressed. He suddenly changed again and God created a new and warm relationship between us. Ronit's parents visited us too and they became very friendly with my own parents. We were very encouraged by the new unity in our family.

Dad suddenly started asking us lots of questions about our faith. I could now explain to him about Yeshua without him getting angry or upset.

We decided that in addition to the wedding ceremony at the Rabbinate we would also arrange for a messianic celebration at Yad-Hashmona village near Jerusalem. I explained to Dad that there we would sing, pray and hear a message on the meaning of marriage in God's eyes. 'That's very good,' responded Dad. I was amazed at the change in him. This wasn't the same man I had known for most of my life!

Three days after our wedding my father died of a heart attack. On that very last day of his life as he was leaving home for work in the morning he told Mum that he had forgiven my brother for something that had happened between them and that he now wanted to visit him. There really was a tremendous change in him and I trust that he came to believe before his death.

Ronit and I now live in Karmiel in Galilee, a beautiful part of Israel. I work as an architectural engineer and we are both active in the small local congregation in our town.

We are Israelis and we love our people. I serve in the reserves and see myself as a real Jew. We have mezuzoth on our door-posts and keep kashrut and all the feasts. We identify with our people and culture and don't want to be a stumbling block to anyone—orthodox or secular. Our door is open and we want all to feel at home with us.

Rabbinic Judaism, like other religions, relies on outward ceremonies and regulations to change man's nature gradually for the better. Man tries to win favour and acceptance with God by his own efforts. He tries to merit eternal life and salvation. But this is a hopeless and fruitless endeavour.

Yeshua on the other hand offers us a simple solution. 'Give me your heart,' he says. 'I have already done all that is needed for you. My sacrifice purifies you and grants forgiveness and new birth. It puts a new heart within you.'

How easy it is to accept his offer, and at the same time how difficult! For the person who has despaired of himself there is nothing easier than accepting this offer gratefully. For a proud and self-reliant person however it can be the toughest thing in the world. We need humility and submission in order to believe in Yeshua and accept what he offers us with such great love. Ronit and I both arrived at this point and can truthfully say that it changed our lives.

# 2

# Shira—A Kibbutz Girl
# Finds the Messiah

*The orthodox guy* jumped onto a chair and shouted into the crowd: 'Hey friends, silence! Listen! Shira believes in God!' His face shone with joy. The other members of the Chabad group were happy too. Their visit to the kibbutz had not been in vain. Shira, this troublesome twelve-year-old girl, who had argued with them so aggressively, now publicly declared her faith in the creator.

Once a year on Yom Kippur, the Day of Atonement, messengers from Chabad village near Tel-Aviv would come to our kibbutz to erect a temporary synagogue, gather a minyan, and recite the solemn prayers on this holiest day of the Jewish calendar. In the evening, after prayers, the kibbutz youngsters would gather to talk and discuss with them matters of religion and faith.

That year I had also joined in the discussions. During the evening I became convinced that there must be some supreme force that created the world and I said so. Actually, I wanted to add: 'But how do I know that this force is your God, and not the Muslim or Christian God?' But the young man in his excitement interrupted me with his loud declaration of my faith. In the ensuing tumult I forgot my question.

I was born in 1964 in Kibbutz Ein-Carmel which is situated in the fertile narrow plain between Mt Carmel and the Mediterranean Sea. My parents were both born in Israel, members of families originally from Poland. My mother comes from a family which boasts of a line of famous Hassidic Rabbis going back to the renowned Rabbi of Kozsck. Her father was brought up in the traditional orthodox 'Cheder', but he later rebelled against the traditions, joined a Zionist movement and made Aliyah to Israel.

My parents met each other whilst on Kibbutz Malkiah in upper Galilee. My mother says that they first met in the home of a mutual friend. It was only at their second meeting that she could determine the colour of his eyes, when he finally lifted his gaze from counting the number of tiles in the floor! They were married in Malkiah, and then moved to Ein-Carmel a short while before I was born.

My parents are secular liberals. For them Judaism is much more than a religion—it includes nationality, culture, folklore and tradition. They are also agnostics, and claim they simply can't know whether God exists, as there is no evidence either way. To this day I am very grateful for the way they brought me up to think for myself, and never to accept platitudes, but to examine things and make my own choices.

My father was the kibbutz electrician. He later studied electrical engineering and became chief engineer of the kibbutz factories in our area. My mother studied nursing while I was in kindergarten and then became the kibbutz nurse. Later she devoted herself to establishing an old folks home for the elderly kibbutz members. This became her real mission in life.

The kibbutz founders had all been immigrants from Poland. Over the years people from other backgrounds joined, so that today you will find members from most Jewish diasporas. But the prevailing smell in our dining hall is still that of gefillte fish rather than of couscous!

Many people I have met have proudly told me how they left home at an early age and became independent. I think very few can compete with me—I was taken from my parents' home to the children's house at the age of two months! This was the usual process for all babies on the kibbutz. It is only in recent years that Ein-Carmel has changed the system to one where the children remain with their parents till the age of twelve. Actually, growing up with many other children can be quite nice. You learn to be considerate of others and you also learn to be independent and to survive on your own.

During my kindergarten years I would sometimes escape at night to my parents' room and curl up in their bed. In the morning they would take me back to the nursery. My parents were wonderful and I loved them very much—I still love and appreciate them. A friend of mine who is a psychologist claims that I have not yet grown out of the childhood stage where parents are admired above anyone else.

As a child I was crazy about dogs. My parents always said that if I didn't return home from kindergarten or school, they would go to the public square in front of the communal dining-hall where a lot of dogs always congregated. Once they managed to scatter the dogs they would find Shira underneath!

It was pleasant growing up in the pastoral atmosphere of village life with nature all around. I always loved the smell of the nearby sea, of freshly mown grass and of the first rain in autumn. I loved being out of doors and that is why I always wanted to work in the ornamental gardening department rather than in the more feminine jobs such as the children's house or the dining-hall.

On the kibbutz it is customary for school children to do practical work one day a week. I stubbornly demanded to work in the garden, and they finally gave in to my request. I loved weeding and planting flowers and shrubs. I enjoyed being in the open air and smelling the fragrance of nature all around me.

There were some fifteen children in my class at school. I loved studies, especially when given research assignments. I had a good head and other pupils would often turn to me for help with their homework. We had a wonderful teacher in primary school who really taught us how to learn and I enjoyed her lessons. On the other hand I was quite lazy about my homework.

Socially I was never quite 'in', never at the centre of events. I always felt something of an outsider and didn't have any close friends in my class—I don't know why. Outside my class I had good friends with whom I could converse on subjects that really interested me.

As I mentioned at the beginning of this story, at the age of twelve I went to that meeting with the Chabad fellows and agreed that a creator must exist. Having declared my faith in God's existence, they told me I now ought to keep the Sabbath, light candles on the Eve of Sabbath and keep the kashrut regulations. They gave me a list of the exact Sabbath candle lighting times and a book on science and religion. Later they were to send me circular letters about other young people who had become 'penitents', turned to orthodox Judaism and maintained their faith despite the pressures of their secular environment.

For a while I tried to live according to their precepts. I really wanted to be right with God, so I tried keeping the commandments. As I was a vegetarian, it wasn't difficult to keep kashrut. I would faithfully light candles every Eve of Sabbath—I felt there was a sense of beauty in this cere-mony—and I kept the Sabbath as well as I could.

This stage lasted for about six months, and then I started having doubts about the whole thing. Though I was only twelve, I had real and deep questions about God and his existence, questions that troubled me very much. I did not gain any spiritual or emotional satisfaction from keeping the commandments, and many of my questions were left unanswered. I noticed that many traditions were not from the Bible, so had not been directly commanded by God.

Gradually I arrived at the conclusion that if God did exist then he must be a terrible and evil God for allowing the Jewish people to suffer so much over the centuries and especially during the holocaust. At about the same time we were reading at school the story of Abraham offering up Isaac on the altar. This seemed to confirm my impression of God: 'What a cruel thing it was to demand that Abraham kill his son with his own hands.'

So I turned to the opposite extreme. I now convinced myself that faith in God was a primitive stage in the development of humanity. In the distant past men believed in many gods. Gradually they evolved to a faith in one supreme God, and today in our modern world we know that God does not exist at all. Everything in the universe is a product of evolution and its laws.

My parents who are very liberal in their views accepted these extreme changes in my beliefs with great understand-ing. They looked at it all as teenage folly, a normal part of my maturing process. They accepted me as I was with all my ups and downs.

When I was fourteen years old, three new volunteers arrived at our kibbutz: Susanne and Charlotte from Sweden and Elly from Holland. They were given a room in the volunteer quarters.

I had always made friends with our foreign volunteers, mainly because I was not fully integrated with my peers. My parents also liked the foreign volunteers and would often adopt some of them and become their kibbutz parents.

These new girls were assigned to work with my mum, helping her care for the sick and elderly. I also managed to work alongside them for a while in the dining-hall.

These girls were different from all other volunteers we had known before. When I visited them in their room, they would sing beautifully together. Susanne, who was short and chubby, had a wonderful soprano voice. They always treated me with love and kindness. After a while I realised that they believed in God, and not just in God, but in Yeshua of Nazareth.

I had never learnt about Yeshua at school. I had only heard about him from people around me, usually in jokes and sometimes in swear words. I thought to myself: 'What a pity for these nice girls! Their faith is so primitive! They must have accepted it from their parents without thinking about it independently.' I decided it was my duty to convince them of their mistake and to explain to them that in our modern world we had passed the stage of religion and faith.

This was why I started visiting them almost daily. For a year and a half I was a constant visitor in their room and fervently tried to prove to them that they were mistaken in their faith. I can't remember all their answers to my arguments, but I do remember that what impressed me most about them was their quality of life. It was always pleasant to be in their company. There was a tangible atmosphere of peace and harmony in their room that was felt by other visitors too. Although they seemed to be normal girls, quite up-to-date in most things, they seemed to have a remarkable sense of love and unity amongst themselves that I had never experienced before.

At work they were always helping the old and the ill, and seemed to really care for them personally. They would visit their patients after working hours and take time to help them and to listen to their tales of woe.

They demonstrated a quality of life I very much longed for. I tried to imitate them and be as good as they were but to no avail. Visiting the sick bored me to death, and being sensitive to other people's needs demanded too high a price. I was very disappointed with myself and wrote this poem at that time:

> I have discovered there are things
> that must be said
> or at least must be written down.
> Many have told me it will help,
> they did not know how much it hurts!
> I will say it:
> I hate myself,
> hate
> hate
> hate.

Why did they succeed where I failed? This thought bothered me for a long time. I began to suspect that there was someone helping them who wasn't helping me.

They once asked me: 'Shira, do you have a goal in life?' I answered that I didn't have one as yet, but that I was searching and would surely find one. That question really got me thinking. What do I really want in life? What are my goals? What is the meaning of life? You can't ask these questions today without raising a storm of laughter—but the laughter only helps us ignore the need to face up to these fundamental issues.

At the age of fifteen I felt that our Bible lessons at school lacked something. We spent hours investigating the meaning of difficult words, but seemed to ignore the message of the passages we read. I approached our teacher and told her about the three volunteers who had such a special faith in the Tenach and in the New Testament. The teacher suggested I invite them to one of our lessons, and so it happened one day that the three of them turned up in our classroom to attend our Bible study class.

They sang and told us something of their lives. They also opened the Tenach and showed us prophecies concerning the coming of the Messiah. Then they read to us how these prophecies had been fulfilled in the New Testament.

They spoke from their hearts and the pupils listened with interest. The teacher tried to lessen the impact of their words by saying: 'You see children, there are people who believe that the New Testament is a continuation of the Tenach, and they try to convince others of their religion because this strengthens their own faith.'

I continued visiting them daily and started asking them difficult questions: 'How could God allow the holocaust? Who said sexual relationships before or outside of marriage were forbidden? Who said that homosexual relationships were forbidden?' I would spend school hours thinking up questions for them and would then attack them with my questions in the evenings. I sometimes hurt their feelings, but they were always kind to me and made me feel welcome.

Shortly after that Bible lesson someone asked me: 'How about it Shira, do you now believe like them?' I answered: 'Me? Never! Their faith is so primitive.'

I got to the stage where I started asking them more and more questions about their faith. They never initiated a conversation on these subjects, but I was troubled by many queries and doubts and was searching for answers.

Gradually I became convinced that it must be God who helped them lead such a life, and that it was their faith that made them different. I started reading the New Testament in Hebrew, and became convinced that Yeshua had really fulfilled all the prophecies in the Tenach relating to the Messiah. This conclusion frightened me. I now felt that someone was asking me to submit to him and I resisted. I knew that if I put my faith in him I could never turn back, it would be for life. I hesitated because I still wanted to be independent and master of my own life.

Mum invited them to our home for my sixteenth birthday. They sang some songs especially for me and wished me many happy returns. It was a great time and I really enjoyed their company. I was very sad when two weeks later the two Swedish girls left the kibbutz and returned home. Elly, the tall, curly-haired Dutch girl, remained alone in that room.

A fortnight after they had left I sat with Elly in her room. For some reason I felt very angry with God. I told her there was no God and that if he existed he must be evil to allow so much suffering in the world. I really wanted to hurt her that evening. Elly listened and then said quietly: 'Shira, you know that he is there and that he loves you. Now enough of that! Go to bed and before you sleep pray to him.'

I left her and went to my room. Suddenly I was aware of myself in a new way, as though I saw myself in a mirror. I saw how bad I was and I realised that God does indeed exist and that he is good and actually loves me in a personal way. Before falling asleep I prayed and said: 'God, if you are there, and I know you are, and if Yeshua is the Messiah, and I know that he is....' I didn't finish the prayer because I fell asleep!

This prayer was the turning point in my life. It was as though I had opened a door and allowed God to start working in me. From that time on my life changed for the better.

I continued reading daily in the New Testament. I was so eager, I couldn't stop. I remember one day sitting in a bus and reading about the crucifixion for the first time. I burst out crying. I cried because he had died—and I didn't know that he also rose from the dead. As I read on, I reached the passage about the resurrection and I was overjoyed. It was all so real to me, as though I myself was present at that last Passover in Jerusalem, witnessing his death and resurrection.

Some months later, I was invited to some Bible lectures at a messianic centre in Haifa. The lecturer was Dr Louis Goldberg, a messianic Jew from the States. He taught us from the book of Leviticus about the sacrifices in the Tabernacle. He explained how the sacrifices symbolised the atoning death of the Messiah. The sinner brought a pure and perfect animal to the Tabernacle, laid his hands on its head and confessed his sins. His sins were transferred to the sacrificial animal, and the pure life of the innocent sacrifice was transferred to the sinner. The death sentence which the sinner deserved was then borne by the sacrificial animal which was slaughtered and died.

All of a sudden, for the first time in my life, I understood the true meaning of Yeshua's death. I realised that I was the sinner and that Messiah had borne the death sentence I deserved at the hands of a holy God. He is my sacrifice, he is my substitute! This realisation was a real shock to me. I turned to the lecturer and said: 'Do you mean to say that I killed Yeshua?' He noticed my excitement and said gently: 'Yes, Shira, it is true. But do relax.' I couldn't. I repeated over and over : 'But I killed him? I?'

I had heard about the theological discussions concerning who had actually killed Yeshua—the Jews or the Romans? Now I realised that it was all nonsense. I had killed him. I was guilty of his death. We had all sinned and were all guilty of his death.

At that lecture I first understood that he had died in my place. I also realised that he had given me his own life in exchange. I was born again. Although I had never committed any terrible sin, I saw that my life was full of vile little sins and that I desperately needed forgiveness and cleansing. I also realised that Yeshua had paid for me with his own life blood because of his deep personal love for me.

When I spoke about this to my parents, they weren't shocked. They thought that this was another fleeting phenomenon in the process of growing up. Several months later, when they saw that I persisted in my faith, they gently suggested that I see a psychiatrist. I knew that they were really concerned for my welfare and so I agreed.

The psychiatrist they took me to was the top man in his profession in the kibbutz movement. He interviewed me for four hours, asking many questions. He asked me if anyone had pressurised me into donating money or into cutting off any contact with my parents. He was obviously worried that I had fallen in with some dangerous sect.

Finally, after the long conversation, he made up his mind: 'Shira,' he said, 'you're OK. Your head is totally

OK.' He repeated this to my parents and calmed their fears. Before we left he said to me: 'My questions weren't random. I know about this faith. My parents were killed in the holocaust and a believing family hid me and brought me up. They were wonderful people.'

My parents decided they wouldn't argue with me any more. For my part I was quite aggressive towards them for a while in my efforts to convince them. I also told my friends on the kibbutz about my faith—many of them laughed at me. This queer Shira now believes in Yeshua! Others were curious or uninterested, and a few were really hurt, seeing in my faith a betrayal of my people.

That same year we had a very good Bible teacher at high school whom I liked. We were studying the book of Isaiah and we reached chapter 9: 'For to us a child is born, to us a son is given, and the government will be on his shoulders. And he will be called Wonderful Counsellor, Mighty God, Everlasting Father, Prince of Peace.'

The teacher asked us: 'Who do you think Isaiah is talking of?' I lifted my hand and said: 'It is very clear, he is speaking about a real child, a human being, who at the same time is also God himself. He will bring peace.' 'Any other suggestions?' asked the teacher. The classroom was silent. The teacher looked at me and said: 'There once was a Jew who claimed that he was not just a man, but that he was God too. He was born in Bethlehem.' He looked at me again and said: 'How do you explain this, Shira? You believe in God, don't you?' I answered: 'I believe in this Jew.'

There was a tumult in the class. The teacher was an elderly man, and he was so shocked by my answer, I was afraid he would have a heart attack. From that day everyone knew about my faith in Yeshua, and that was good, because now I could talk freely about it and wasn't tempted to hide it.

Six months after I had come to faith Elly returned to Holland. I remained as the only believer on the kibbutz. I continued to read the Scriptures regularly, and I learned a lot during this time on my own. I realised that believers can read and understand the Bible on their own, because God's Spirit is within us. We don't need the authorised commentaries of the sages, as the orthodox claim.

On graduating from high school it was time to be called up for military service. After the initial training, I became an educational NCO. I was responsible for the education and geographical instruction of the unit I was attached to.

It was an interesting job. I led the soldiers on many hikes all over Israel. We also visited places where Yeshua had walked—that was wonderful! I didn't hide my faith but spoke about it to others.

During my service I worked at three different army bases. The best was when I was attached to an artillery unit for six months. The soldiers tended to spoil us few female soldiers. There was a good spirit and we all became fast friends.

I loved planning hikes. It was fun to sit down with a map and plan the route. Then I would go out with just one other person to familiarise myself with it before taking the unit out. I hiked a lot. There is nothing better than taking a backpack and heading out into the countryside. It's a real delight.

Of course I also had frustrations, especially with officers who thought only of exercises and manoeuvres and wouldn't authorise one hour of the soldiers' time for hikes or conversations. They thought I was a nagging headache with a hobby horse and didn't value my services. Other officers encouraged me and gave me all the time and help I needed, so it was a mixed experience.

In every unit in which I served, I felt it my duty to organise the weekly talk between the officer and his men. Some officers were afraid to reveal their true selves to those under them, but this is very important and I always pushed them into doing it.

I wasn't always spiritually strong during my army days. I had my ups and downs, but God helped me to overcome and to persevere. You don't have to have a breakdown in the army. It can actually be a very good time.

One Saturday I stayed at the base. I sat in the office and read the book of Daniel. The phone rang, and when I lifted the receiver a voice said: 'Hello, I'm in bed right now, would you like to join me?' My first reaction was anger and shock. I wanted to slam down the receiver and shut him up. Instead I said:'Do you want to know what I am doing right now? I'm studying the book of Daniel.' 'What for?' he asked in astonishment. I told him about my faith in Yeshua and we chatted about it for almost an hour. Finally he said: 'Thanks, it was good to hear about these things.'

Another time I was on guard duty on the Day of Atonement. I noticed a soldier sitting nearby reading an English book. We started talking, and it turned out that he was an American who had visited Israel, converted to Judaism and then married an Israeli girl. He came from a believing home, but was disappointed by the hypocrisy he saw in their congregation. All that day we spoke about Yeshua.

Quite some time later I happened to meet him in another place. He asked: 'What do you think of the crucifixion? Did the Romans crucify Yeshua or was it the Jews?' I told him about the experience I had when I realised that I had actually killed Yeshua. I told him that in his love for us Yeshua had died for our sins and given us his life. He listened carefully and was silent for a while and I felt slightly embarrassed. Years later a friend told me that he had met him and that he now believed in Yeshua. I was delighted.

After my discharge from the army, I returned to Ein-Carmel and worked there in gardening and with the live-stock. I then spent a year in England at a Bible School and on my return to the kibbutz I worked with pre-nursery age children. It was wonderful working with children, and I loved them very much. After a while in this work, I decided to go to Eilat and work as a volunteer in a messianic youth hostel there. It was really difficult for me to say good-bye to the children I loved so much. They gave me a farewell party, and this is part of a poem I wrote for them for that occasion:

> You don't have to be like me,
> You can be much better
> Because you are loved.
> It is about love I wanted to speak;
> Firstly that I love you
> And think a lot about you.
> This goes without saying.
> If this was the first time
> You heard of it,
> It would be too late.
>
> I want to tell you that I pray
> That love may be your nurse,
> That love may be your motive,
> That it may be your daily bread.
> That you may be love's messengers,
> Giving and receiving love
> That it may fill your days and nights.
>
> Yes, Love is another name for God.

When I left the kibbutz, several members told me how sorry they were that I was leaving, because they really liked me. I was touched, as it was quite a change in their attitude towards me.

I have no lucrative profession and am not yet married. Mum is worried for me and recently wrote: 'What are you doing with your life? Why don't you use your gifts to the full? Why don't you get married? You are missing out on the most beautiful thing in the world—having a husband and children.'

I wrote back: 'Without God, maybe a husband and children are the most wonderful thing in the world, though I doubt it. I have seen too many couples with deep marital problems. But when you know Yeshua, there is nothing better in the whole world. No man and no baby can give me what Yeshua gives.'

I am now working as a guide with the Nature Preservation Society. Israel in the spring-time is a glorious sight—full of green and of wild flowers. I could gaze on it forever. I have returned to my first love.

Believing does not mean that we lead a problem-free life. But in Yeshua we do find fulfilment of all our longings. When we submit to him and devote ourselves to his service he gives us true satisfaction and true peace, which no one else can give.

I have a friend with whom I have been sharing my faith for several years. She has repeatedly told me that she knows that what I say is the truth—but she always puts off her personal decision. Her life is one long story of mistakes and of falls. Only Yeshua can help her. I recently gave her these words:

Hannah, have you closed yet another gate?
Why can't you hear him call your name?
You who have tasted of grief and death,
And once almost knelt down to give him yourself.

Hannah, you are walking down the same lane again,
Seeking for love in a man's embrace.
You should remember where it leads you.
Why reject Yeshua who patiently waits?

He died for you on the cross,
For you he felt the nails and the pain.
Today he calls you again and again,
But you ignore it—and kill him again.

Disappointment will come instead of love.
You have paid, you are hungry,
You almost died neglected and alone,
High on drugs, wasted from within,
Murdered your children, punished yourself.

Don't you hear him still calling your name?
The only one who can give you all
Still loves, still willing to forgive.
He never hurts, your suffering he bears.

Hannah, he calls—can't you hear him shout?
Reach out your hand to him before you drown!

# 3

# Israel Segal—An Officer
# Finds Peace

*I was born in 1937* in a small village in Romania to Jewish parents who kept the traditions but were not orthodox. My mother was a pious woman who loved God and fervently prayed to him. She instilled in me the belief that God exists and that he rewards men according to their deeds.

My father was a merchant, a man of the world, always busy and preoccupied with his work. Both parents always had to work very hard to make ends meet. Life for them was a constant struggle for existence, and they had no strength left to satisfy their children's emotional needs.

From my earliest childhood the world always seemed to be a dull and a dark place, hostile and dangerous. Even when the sun shone outside and the skies were clear and blue, our home seemed to be shrouded in a cloud of despondency. I was always glad when the day ended and was never happy to see a new day dawn.

The Second World War was another dark cloud over my childhood. Anti-semitism was rampant, we were forced to

47

wear the yellow badge and experienced hunger and fear. Constant bombing attacks added to the trauma. We slept in unfurnished rooms, their window panes shattered, freezing with the cold. We learned to steal potatoes and fruit from the market to survive. We children sometimes dared to taunt the German soldiers but as Jews we lived in constant fear of being deported to the death camps.

Sometimes I would climb some tall trees in our neighbourhood to watch the bombers diving over the nearby city of Botosani. One such day as I sat in the tree-top a bomb landed close by. The blast made me lose my balance and I fell down and broke my arm. There was no plaster available, so the bandage was set in cow's dung! My elbow is still slightly deformed from that strange treatment.

I was eight years old when the war finally ended, but the longed-for peace didn't bring us any real joy. The new communist regime promised equality for all and improved living standards for the working class, but in reality it was a regime of terror and oppression. All real or fancied enemies of the regime were thrown into prisons and concentration camps, tortured and killed. It was only by using these cruel methods that the regime succeeded in surviving for forty-four long years until the downfall of Ceaucescu in December 1989.

The economic situation worsened instead of improving. We were down to our last resources and experienced real hunger pangs. My father felt forced to try his luck on the black market buying and selling food, and lived in constant fear of his activities being disclosed to the authorities.

I grew up in these difficult years with seemingly endless problems dampening my spirit. As a result I was often depressed and suffered from a serious lack of self-esteem and from an inferiority complex. I was sure that I had no talents worth speaking of, that I was ugly and that I couldn't catch up with my peers at school. I was also constantly worried about the future: how would I make a living? What profession would I learn? Would I get married and have a family? Would I be able to make ends meet? I was in a constant state of anxiety and worry and depression. Why was I born and what am I living for? I could only see troubles all around me. Life seemed very dull and offered me no pleasure whatsoever.

I joined the Comsomol, the communist youth movement and was a member for five years. I decided to hide my emotional problems behind a facade of self-assured cockiness. This play-acting in the youth group plus the brain-washing I received there only served to increase my problems. I came to loathe myself and my people and all enemies of communism. They taught us to despise the weak and to worship the party and the leaders of party and state. This was part of the personality cult that was being forced on the Romanian people.

The authorities eventually got to know of my father's black market deals. He was very scared of being arrested and as a way of escape he decided to apply for an exit visa for our family to emigrate to Israel. Amazingly our visas were soon granted and in the autumn of 1950 we found ourselves on board the Romanian ship 'Transylvania' sailing from Konstanza on the Black Sea towards the Mediterranean and Israel.

The weather was delightful and the sea was calm. It could have been a wonderful time for me but I couldn't enjoy myself. Years of brain-washing and inculcated suspicion made me look for a way to serve the authorities whilst gaining some advantage for myself. In return for a good daily meal in the crew's galley I was assigned to guard a certain passageway and keep the passengers out of it. This gave me a feeling of power and of being on the side of the authorities. I could hurt those weaker than myself and even prevented my younger brother from enjoying a stroll on the deck.

The destructive effects of communist education did not disappear overnight. They haunted me for a long time. This kind of education turns innocent children into evil monsters eager to betray their own parents and close relatives and willing to torment the weak in the misguided belief of thereby serving the interests of party and state.

Finally we arrived at Haifa and I was thrilled with the experience of a new country and of freedom. The day after arrival however found me in my usual depressed state of mind. The burning sun and the hot dry 'Chamsin' desert winds of September coupled to the countless mosquitoes which seemed uniquely attracted to my untanned skin, quickly served to dampen any initial enthusiasm I might have felt.

After several weeks of waiting we were assigned to a transit camp near Migdal-Ashkelon on the southern Mediterranean coast. Immediately on arrival we were given a tent and my parents registered us at the local primary school where we started to learn Hebrew in addition to the regular curriculum.

I explored our new surroundings. I especially loved to wander around the sand dunes that stretched between our camp and the sea. I enjoyed wading in the clear cool Mediterranean water, which wasn't yet polluted by industry. I would pick figs and other fruit off the trees in the deserted orchards of the Arab population of Migdal who had fled the area during the War of Independence. It was a good time for me.

Winter came and with it heavy downpours of rain. Our large tent hardly leaked and we were reasonably dry though quite cold. My father and the other men were employed in building apartment blocks into which we were eventually moved when all the building work was completed.

As usual I wasn't happy with my lot. I always harboured the sneaking suspicion that the grass on the other side must be greener and that I was missing out on something. I felt a deep longing for something I lacked but which I couldn't define. I searched for it in books, amongst family and friends, but I never found it. That feeling kept constantly nagging at me and made me perpetually restless.

I observed our religious neighbours who dressed in traditional black suits, wore the kippah and the tallit and regularly attended synagogue for prayers. They seemed to be fulfilling all of God's commandments but their demeanour and behaviour revealed that they too lacked peace and joy. I decided that religion had nothing to offer me and that it could not fill the void within me.

I looked for another solution and made enquiries into the possibilities of attending a kibbutz school. The 'Youth Aliya' organisation accepted me and after some training in one of their institutions I was transferred to a boarding school in Kibbutz Beit-Zera.

Feelings of restlessness and of loneliness followed me into the kibbutz. I couldn't rid myself of them. Even though I slept in a room with three other kids and worked all day with other people I never felt that I really belonged or that I was really accepted.

I was so restless that I couldn't stick to one job for any length of time. I would be assigned to the dairy, switch over to field produce department then on to the vegetable garden and back again in a vicious circle. I always hoped to find fulfilment in something new and different. I was always sure that the really interesting and exciting things happened in the other departments, but when I got there I was disappointed and discovered it was all just more of the same—'there is nothing new under the sun!' Then I would try to get back to my previous job and run through the whole cycle again.

I finally got fed up with myself and my emotional instability and recurring crises. I decided to return home for a while hoping that there I would be rid of them.

I left the kibbutz and returned home in 1952 with the primary school certificate in my pocket. I now faced the challenge of choosing an occupation and training for it. I registered at a vocational high school in Rehovot and in September 1952 I started my studies there.

In Rehovot I lived in a tiny rented room that had no shower or toilet facilities—they were both in the yard outside. I had to work for my living as my parents couldn't help me. Every evening after school hours I worked in a garage from five to ten for a tiny wage. Every morning from six-thirty to nine-thirty I would milk cows on a neighbouring farm belonging to an orthodox family for an even smaller wage.

My daily diet consisted of bread and jam or bread and sardines. During school hours I was tired and hungry and couldn't concentrate on my vocational or theoretical studies. I was the only pupil in my class who had to work for his living and who didn't have proper facilities for doing his homework. My feelings of inferiority deepened.

My room was located in the Marmurek suburb of Rehovot which was populated mainly by Jews from the Yemen. They were really nice people but their children had developed a deep dislike of Ashkenazis. When they discovered me living right there amongst them they considered me their rightful prey and started harassing me. I searched for alternative routes into our area to avoid the streets where they would lie in wait for me, but to no avail.

They always seemed to find me and I would return to my room nursing a black eye and bruised all over.

Quite close by was a boarding institute for girls. Feeling very lonely and being influenced by the movies I occasionally saw I tried to find some solace and companionship with one of the girls there. The area toughs soon found out about our relationship. Whether out of jealousy or out of plain nastiness they decided to teach me a lesson. One day on my return from a visit there a large gang of them ambushed me and set on me with fists and sticks. I desperately tried to defend myself but in vain; they were too many for me. My strength ebbed and I fell down. They finally left me and went away. I examined myself all over and found that my face was all swollen, two front teeth were broken and I was bruised and bleeding all over—but I was alive! I barely managed to crawl back to my room where I had to nurse myself as best I could.

I had no money for dental treatment and that was depressing. I slowly recovered my strength and was filled with a burning desire for revenge. I exercised in an effort to strengthen my muscles and fists. Within a short time I had the opportunity of taking my revenge on one of the leaders of that gang, the worst guy of the lot. For weeks after that encounter he walked around with a patch over his eye.

I continued attending school feeling inferior and embittered. I decided that I had to compensate with hard work and perseverance what I couldn't achieve otherwise. It was a hard slog—others seemed to grasp things so much more easily than I did and seemed to have all the advantages. From time to time I got involved in scrapes and troubles of various kinds such as cribbing in the exams. To my surprise I was hardly ever caught or punished and attributed it to my good luck. I finally managed to pass all the exams and graduated from that school in 1956.

That same year in August I was conscripted into the army and taken to boot camp just two months before the outbreak of the Sinai campaign.

In the army I finally found the good life I had always looked for. Even boot camp felt like a five-star hotel to me! There was an abundance of food for the first time in my life. Who can count the endless plates of porridge I devoured. And I would always hurry back to stand in the line and ask for more. This was the life I had always dreamed about. The army became everything to me: home, family, adventure, excitement and entertainment all in one package deal. I had now found it all and life wasn't dull or boring any more.

After my three years of regular service I decided to sign up for another two years in the professional army. I really enjoyed my time there. I felt fulfilled and proud of my work and for the first time in my life I had a real salary.

Towards the end of these two years my old restlessness started to reassert itself. I felt a strong urge to travel around the world and discover new horizons. I wanted to see new countries and the far-away places I had only seen in films. Immediately on being discharged I went to sea on board the freighter 'Ampal' as a machine-room rating. The ship displaced some fifteen thousand tons and it was sailing to the Far East.

I will never forget the shock of that first experience on the unreliable oceans. Storms and typhoons hit us and the ship was tossed about like a toy in the huge seas with waves over ten metres high. I suffered intense seasickness with that terrible feeling of nausea that never seems to abate or to leave you.

I did enjoy visiting the exotic ports and experiencing new cultures, but I soon realised that all thrills came to an end after an hour or two and I would be left hankering for more of the same.

I was really terrified of the wild sea with its unpredictable fierce storms, winds and waves. I just couldn't get used to it. After spending a year sailing the seas I returned with a feeling of great relief to my first love—the army.

Life in the army was full of activity. I joined an elite unit where I could release my pent-up energy and satisfy my longing for adventure. On the whole I was a disciplined and loyal soldier who always respected authority and those higher in rank—a leftover of my communist days. I obeyed orders and worked very hard.

By 1967 I felt that it was time for me to get married and establish a family. As a career soldier I was relatively well off and I longed for the warmth and comradeship I felt family life could offer.

I first met Zivah in the army. After a brief time of acquaintance we got married in 1967. Right from the beginning of our marriage I decided that this must be a serious matter. We would sincerely care for each other and enjoy a loving and faithful relationship. No wild parties and no merry socialising for us, I decided! We had good intentions but they didn't take us far nor did they last very long.

The Six Day War broke out soon after our wedding. It was over within a week. It was an overwhelming victory with relatively few casualties. By the end of the war the old city of Jerusalem with the Western Wall was in our hands, as well as the Golan Heights, Judea and Samaria, the Gaza strip and all of the Sinai peninsula.

Those were heady days for us. The generals who had seemed so worried at the outbreak of hostilities now proudly slapped each other's backs. A wave of excitement and enthusiasm swept over the country. We were all caught up in this state of euphoria and self-confidence that would later take its toll.

The years now seemed to fly past. We had two children who kept my wife busy whilst I was caught up in the whirl of military duties. I changed jobs and rose in the ranks. I was sent to Idi Amin's Uganda to help train its army. Though we were put up in a luxury hotel and offered caviar to eat I didn't feel at ease. Something was wrong and rotten in that set-up and I was glad to be called back to Israel just prior to the Yom Kippur War in 1973.

This war caused real trauma to many of us veteran soldiers. We saw tens of our tanks go up in flames. At the base of Rephidim we saw rows of dead bodies lying covered with blankets except for the black or red boots sticking out from underneath them. We saw boys' faces ringed with curls, their smiles frozen forever by death. It was tragic. The heroic stories of that war faded into insignificance compared with the sorrow of bereavement we experienced as we shared the sad news with their families, and compared with the terrible sight of shattered bodies and limbs on the battlefield.

The officers moved about worried by the uncertainty of the situation. Communication difficulties kept us from always having an up-to-date picture of what was happening in other areas.

This war was a difficult experience for all of us. It caused a changed perspective on life for many soldiers and officers. I noticed that immediately after the war the synagogues were again filled with people attending prayers, many of whom had never set a foot in a synagogue before. But two years later everything was forgotten and people returned to their idols of materialism and nationalism as though the war had never taken place.

After the war we started having family problems. My

wife believed in total liberty and permissiveness and began having affairs with other men. When I protested she demanded a divorce. For the sake of our young children I agreed not to interfere with her any more and she carried on as she liked.

As a result of the war I felt deep emotional fatigue. Experiencing death to such a degree made me a softer man. The militant spirit I had known before disappeared and my attitudes to those under my command changed. The enthusiasm I had felt during my seventeen years of service was gone. I decided to participate in a nine-month army medic course as a preparation for a possible change to civilian life.

I became more concerned for the welfare of young soldiers and tried to do my best for them, urging them to attend more courses and to sign up for careers with the army. I wanted to help build a better, more effective and morally stronger army.

My family life was by now completely ruined. We behaved as total strangers to each other. Zivah took care of the children and I supported them financially. We had no relationship beyond that. Zivah nagged more and more about a divorce and I finally gave in to her wishes. We got a legal divorce which gave her custody of the children. I left home with a bag of clothes under my arm, never to return again.

Out of the frustrations and the emotional upheavals of that time there grew in me a longing to know the true meaning of life and I started on a quest for some spiritual experience of knowing God.

My final assignment in the army took me to South Lebanon where I got to know Christian soldiers in the South Lebanon Army of Major Sa'ed Haddad. There were also American volunteers in the area doing social work and I became quite friendly with one of them. We sometimes toured the area together and one day he asked if I would like to visit a neighbouring kibbutz with him. I agreed and after a short drive I found myself in a small room where some twenty young foreign volunteers were seated in a circle.

They sang some nice songs and prayed together. I was struck by their seriousness and by the sincerity of their prayers. These youngsters seemed to have a direct relationship with God. What was their secret? They seemed so different to other Christians I knew.

During my time in South Lebanon we also helped a Christian organisation set up a radio station called 'Voice of Hope' which broadcasts specifically to the Christian community in Lebanon which was engaged in the bloody civil war for so long. Later on, a TV station was added and its broadcasts could be picked up in all surrounding countries including Israel.

This was how I first met a different kind of Christian, 'believers' they called themselves, and these chance acquaintances influenced my life and prepared me for things to come.

In 1981 I was pensioned from the service with the rank of Lieutenant Colonel and given the usual holiday at army expense which officers receive on discharge.

On a bright and very warm day I found myself driving my Renault 4 southwards towards Sharm el Sheikh at the tip of the Sinai peninsula. I wanted to say farewell to the vast expanses of the desert I had grown to love during my times of service there.

As I reached Dahab I noticed the lone figure of a young blond man walking towards the Bedouin village carrying a jerry can in each hand. It was noon with the sun directly overhead and the temperature at least forty degrees centigrade in the shade.

I stopped the car and beckoned to him. He approached me somewhat hesitantly obviously wondering what this high-ranking officer in the car wanted of him. I asked him where he was heading and he said that he had been to the Moshav to get water for himself and was now heading back to the Bedouin village where he lived. I offered him a lift and we drove on towards the Bedouin village some three kilometres away.

On the way he introduced himself. 'My name is Johan and I'm from Holland,' he said. He invited me to come into his booth for a glass of tea. I parked the car outside his makeshift shanty and entered the coolness of the shaded booth. I liked this fellow and wondered if it would be possible to stay on for a while here and enjoy some swimming and diving.

We sat in the booth and talked as I sipped at the glass of tea he offered me. Suddenly someone poked his head into the narrow entrance and asked: 'Johan, do you have any water?' The young man didn't hesitate but gave the caller one of his jerry cans.

A few moments later someone else turned up and asked for water. The second jerry can followed in the wake of the first. 'This fellow must be crazy!' I thought to myself. 'He walks three kilometres in each direction in this dreadful heat to get some water for himself and then he gives it away to all these lazy bums on the beach of the Bedouin village!'

I sipped thoughtfully at the glass of tea in my hand. Instead of the five minutes I had promised to stay in his booth I sat there for hours talking to him.

Towards evening Johan distributed the food he had in the booth to people on the beach. He then picked up his guitar and sang some folk songs. I liked this and fetched my

mouth-organ from the car to accompany him in singing
'Jerusalem of Gold'. He then sang some other songs I
didn't recognise and finished off by reading a passage from
the Bible.

I stayed the night in his booth. As I was falling asleep I
wondered about this fellow Johan. What motivated him?
He seemed so kind and genuine and willing to help others.
What was his secret?

Instead of the five minutes I had originally intended to
spend with him, I remained with Johan in the Bedouin
village at Dahab for three whole weeks. He sang and read
from the Bible daily to those on the beach. He also took
care of the Bedouin children, dressing their wounds and
telling them Bible stories, and helped the travellers on the
beach in any way he could. We had lots of time in which to
talk and discuss the meaning of life. We soon became firm
friends.

One day, sitting alone on the beach, I suddenly grasped
that I could have a personal relationship with God only
through faith in Yeshua, the Messiah of whom Johan
spoke. He had given up his life for me to atone for my sins.
I hadn't read the Tenach or the New Testament, but sitting
out there on the beach I felt as though a streak of lightning
had suddenly managed to pierce the darkness of my life.
This then was the secret, the key to the personal relationship with God I had so often longed for.

I felt a deep sense of joy and inner peace flooding over
me such as I had never felt before. It was like being on a
honeymoon with God himself who loved me and cared for
me. I did not know much about him, I did not know if all
persons coming to faith had this same experience, but I
simply rejoiced in what had happened to me and I felt like a
man born anew.

During my remaining time in Dahab I came to understand that Yeshua is really God revealed in human form as predicted by the prophets in the Tenach. I was not troubled by theological questions, but I noticed a real change in myself. The heaviness was gone and I had real peace and joy. I became more tolerant of others and I felt a deeper love for my people Israel. I even started to like the orthodox people who up to that point had always put me off.

I returned home and looked for a job. I prayed that I would find a job abroad and was soon offered one by a company that sent me to Nigeria as a senior administrator with a salary three times my army one. But after a month there I realised it was not my place. I had no peace and felt so miserable that I even wept and cried to God for his help. Finally I approached the chief engineer who was my superior and he agreed to release me from my contract without demanding any compensation. He even authorised a flight ticket back to Israel at company expense, which included a stopover in Paris.

I decided not to return immediately to Israel but to make use of the stopover in Paris for a break in Europe. I ended up travelling around Europe for six months and even reached the Far East after that.

Although I now believed in God I did not know how to find his guidance and direction for my life. I didn't read the Bible and I acted quite irresponsibly and got into some dangerous situations whilst travelling around.

My last stop was in Japan. When I went in for a visa extension I was surprised to be met by a point blank refusal. This had never happened to me before. I have no doubt it was God's hand taking me back to Israel at exactly the right time. My father had just died and the family expected me back for his funeral. I had also applied for a place at a nursing school some time before and they had now fixed an interview date which I must not miss.

I flew back to Israel and attended my father's funeral. Some days later I went for the interview at the nursing school. I was quite sure of myself, after all I was a high-ranking officer with an image of efficiency and ability. I had also attended the nine-month course for army medics whilst in the army.

There were three ladies on the interviewing committee. I recognised one of them as a high official in the ministry of health. She turned to me and said that from her point of view I wasn't suitable for the nursing profession. I was stunned by her words but outwardly kept up a self-assured and confident facade. The rejection in her voice pained me and I silently prayed to God as I waited for the final verdict.

Some minutes later I was called back into the room and told that I had been accepted and that I should register quickly as there was only one more free place on this course!

I was overjoyed. I knew that God had intervened. I later realised that it was my rank that had bothered them. They weren't sure that I could adapt to the menial tasks of nursing such as washing patients, emptying bed pans or attending to the terminally ill.

I hurried off to register and soon after started my studies. I liked the subject matter and felt fulfilment at the knowledge that I was in the right place.

Some time later the nursing school organised a Purim party for students and staff. During the party I went up to the podium and sang some messianic songs I had recently learnt. The response wasn't overwhelming, but when I had finished a student nurse named Malka came up to me and asked me about these songs. She had never heard such tunes before. I explained that these were messianic songs and after the party was over we sat and chatted. I told her of my faith in Yeshua as the Messiah and gave her a brief account of my journey to faith.

'Why must I always meet the craziest guys in the world?' Malka asked herself as she returned to her room that evening. Out of that chance meeting our friendship developed. Six months after that party I invited her to accompany me to a messianic congregation and she agreed. She joined me that Sabbath and then started attending the services regularly. She finally came to faith in Yeshua and I was very happy for her.

The nursing course drew to its end and Malka and I decided to get married. God provided us both with good jobs and took care of all our needs. We now have two children—a boy, Yinnon and a girl, Muriel, and are expecting our third.

Yeshua has truly brought me into the rest I had always longed for. Above all else I now have a direct and personal relationship with him. I now understand that the restlessness I had experienced since childhood and the desperate search for new experiences were actually a search for God himself. Only God could heal the wounds inflicted by my difficult childhood and by life's many problems and only he could fill the void within me.

It is wonderful to look back on my life and see God's providence. For many years he kept me safe and led me even though I did not know him. I called it luck. I always seemed to have luck in the many dangers I've been through and I have always been kept from the worst possible results of my follies and mistakes. God was the one who in his grace and mercy always lifted me out of the pits I had dug for myself through my sins. An invisible hand seemed to protect and guide me.

All my life I have been interested and intrigued by the wonders of creation but for most of my life I had ignored the much more wonderful Creator of it all. I had expected to find peace and joy in new experiences, places and adventures but had never found them there. Only when I believed in Yeshua the Messiah who gave his life as a sacrifice for me did I receive that wonderful inner peace and assurance that now accompany me wherever I go.

I was deeply sorry for all the wasted years of my life, sorry for all my sins and failures. But I thank God for the forgiveness I found in Yeshua. I am fully assured that he forgave my sins and blotted them out as though they had never happened.

Gradually I learned to be diligent in my Bible reading and study. I learned to pray regularly and to ask for his direction and will for my life. Through this process I grew in the faith and received his power to resist pressures and temptations.

Today my purpose in life is to serve God and to bring him glory in all I do. I have discovered that Yeshua the Messiah is the way, the truth and the life. I thank God for taking me out of terrible darkness and bringing me into his wonderful light. My prayer is that this story of my life will help others to find the key to a new life.

# 4

# Maja—From Atheism to Faith

*My parents came* to Israel from Yugoslavia in 1950. They were atheists who did not believe in God or in the Bible and I was brought up in this anti-religious atmosphere.

Even as a little child I felt that my parents did not understand me. It wasn't that they were harsh with me, they were actually quite loving and kind, but I was extremely sensitive and very hurt when they were unable to make the effort to open up their hearts to my emotions and thoughts.

At an early age I decided that I would shut myself up into my own world and keep my emotional distance from my parents. I decided to chart my own life without them, and so right throughout my childhood and teens I spent a lot of time on my own, isolated, brooding on my own feelings and thoughts—and reading books.

Nahariya at that time was still a nice little town near the sea. When I got into high school, we had a bad time with terrorists attacking from the sea and firing Katyusha rockets at Nahariya from within Lebanon. Sometimes you could hear the whine of the rocket before it landed and you wondered if this time it was going to hit you. We spent hours in the air-raid shelters. It was all part of growing up in Nahariya. During the Yom Kippur War we high school pupils volunteered to help in hospitals, in delivering mail and in other essential services.

In my teens I was rebellious and looked for adventure. I was frustrated and felt that there was something missing in life; there didn't seem to be any sense or meaning to it. At the same time I also paradoxically saw much beauty and many enjoyable things around me. I tried drugs and searched for other experiences. There were many good things in life that I enjoyed, but always deep down I had this existential pain, this 'Weltschmerz' that I couldn't define.

I searched for meaning in life, for satisfactory answers to my many questions, but couldn't find any. I looked into different avenues such as psychology, scientology and other world views. There were always things I agreed with, but never a total answer. It was as though I wandered around in a thick forest seeing only individual trees with no apparent order or system.

After high school, in 1975, I was called into the army and assigned to the communications corps. After doing several courses, I was sent to Sharm el Sheikh at the southernmost tip of Sinai where I spent most of my service.

I really fell in love with the Sinai peninsula—the desert, the beaches, the wilderness. It had a very special atmosphere about it that I loved.

On my days off I would travel around Sinai—Santa Katarina, Nueiba, Dahab—I was drunk with the desert atmosphere and I loved travelling around the wide spaces. It was so relaxing after the rigid military discipline.

One holiday I spent at the beach at Dahab with some friends. We behaved like real travellers opting out of bourgeois society and taking a break from life on the sandy beach.

We met a blond Dutch fellow there, Johan, who dressed like a Bedouin and walked around distributing Bibles and other literature. I got friendly with his sister Nelly who was out there on a visit. His religious talk didn't interest me in the least, but I was struck with his friendliness and the way he shared the little food he had with all of us.

On being released from the army I registered at the Hebrew University in Jerusalem to study biology. On the surface my life and my future looked promising: I had talents and ability and if I could finish university I would have a successful career staked out for me.

However, the truth was that I had registered as a result of my parent's pressure to do so. They expected me to head in this direction. I was so engrossed in my search for meaning and purpose in life, I had so many unanswered questions, that I was unable to concentrate on my studies. I missed many lectures, taking off every now and then to go to the Sinai for a break, and I finally dropped out of university completely without even finishing my first year.

Like many young Israelis I had always dreamt of travelling abroad. I now found work in a bank in order to save up for my planned trip. Actually it was a good job and I could have stayed on and made a career of it, but I only wanted the money for travel, and so after a year and a half of work I resigned and sailed from Haifa to Greece with a good friend of mine. Our plan was to travel through Yugoslavia on to Germany. This was in 1980 and I was twenty-three at the time.

The girl I had teamed up with was a close friend I had

known since we were children and she had the same urge to travel as I had. We were sure we would get on fine together. I realised we might have some conflicts along the way but was sure I could handle any problem. I was very self-confident at the time.

Not long into the trip we had some arguments over silly things that caused tensions between us. We didn't know how to deal openly with such matters and so finally, when we arrived in Germany, things came to a head and we split up in anger. This unexpected conflict left me really shattered, with many questions about myself and doubts about my views and beliefs. I continued on my own and after two months of travel I reached Amsterdam.

This was a dream come true. It is a lovely city with beautiful architecture, music and art. There was an atmosphere of freedom, it was very colourful and there were lots of young people milling around doing their own thing. It was very attractive and made me forget my troubles for a while. Later I did manage to see through the superficial beauty to the deep pain and suffering of the drug addicts and others in this lovely city.

I lodged in cheap hostels until I met a group of young Hungarians who lived in derelict houses. I made friends with them and joined them. Later I discovered that they were addicted to heroin and I watched their agony when they couldn't obtain the drug. I also realised that they not only begged for money but would also steal it when desperate for the heroin they could no longer live without.

One morning I discovered that some of my money had been stolen from me whilst I slept. I was very hurt by this betrayal of trust amongst friends, and this ugly experience brought on a state of depression in me. It was winter-time when everything looks grey and cold, there was no sun to be seen, and I felt there was no hope. It was as if I was in a nightmare where time had no meaning and there seemed to be no exit from this dark hole.

I remembered having seen an ad for a cheap hostel at the railway station. I copied the address and found the youth hostel 'The Shelter' which was situated right in the middle of the red light district of Amsterdam.

In the midst of the squalor and suffering that I saw in that area, this place stood out in a unique way. The staff were all honest and highly moral people who loved helping others. I felt at ease in their company, it was like returning home to a safe haven. They all believed in Yeshua—but that didn't disturb me, even though I was cynical of their faith.

I decided to do something about the depression I was in, to do some sightseeing, find a job. I was offered a job in the hostel helping with the housework which I gladly accepted. I used the hostel as a base and continued living my own life. I did not form any deep relationships with the staff, even though Edith and Tros, the Dutch people in charge of the hostel, treated me very kindly.

I was glad they did not ask me to attend their lectures and prayer times. I wondered how such seemingly intelligent people could believe those myths about God and about Yeshua.

I had many discussions with Michelle, a work-mate who was a believer. I tried to prove to her that the kind of God described in the Bible simply didn't exist. There were only energies, nature, random processes. Science and psychology had an answer to all phenomena, and religious faith was simply a straw that drowning people clutched at. Of course I had to listen to her arguments too, and slowly the thought pushed itself into my consciousness: 'What if all this is true—how would it affect reality?' The answers I had received were new and strange. They involved a mode of existence unknown to me, but I had to admit that the possibility at least existed and that the arguments had their own internal logic.

I also realised that although I came from a secular background I had an irrational opposition to Yeshua and his claims. This was due to my Jewish background that subconsciously influenced my thinking and emotions. I tried to overcome this inhibition and to examine this faith objectively and discover whether it was true. At the outset of this task I was pretty sure it was all a mistake.

These conversations and my internal struggles went on for some two months after which I came to the conclusion that God does exist and that Yeshua must be the Messiah. I discovered tremendous depth in the Bible, and found that the Genesis description of creation offered a viable theory with its own logic for explaining the world as we know it. System and order seemed be emerging in the tangled forest I had lived in.

I now believed in the existence of God: that he had created the world and that he was the God that the Bible described. I also came to accept the biblical view of man as a sinner standing before a holy God. The sacrifices of the Tenach now took on a new meaning, and I began to understand my Jewish roots. I tried hard to fight against these new discoveries, I would bring up counter-arguments to negate them, but always returned to the same conclusions. I also realised the full implications of these ideas—that if this was really so, I couldn't live as before, motivated only by forces centred on myself and on my comfort, my life would have to undergo a drastic change.

As I thought and read and discussed these matters, I realised that I was being changed from within in a strange way by some power outside of myself that could not just be blind and random chance. I was conscious at various levels of my being, understanding, emotions and experience that this was something much bigger, that this must be God himself working in me and changing the very depths of my being. I needed finally to acknowledge him.

I remember one afternoon when I was resting in my room and thinking of the great change that had come over me in such a brief time. I acknowledged that it was the finger of God—I had been drowning in life's morass, but he in his love reached out his hand and pulled me out of the mud, the pain, the sorrow, out of suffering and sin. That moment I felt a wave of love for God overwhelming me. With tears in my eyes I finally came to the point where I thanked him for all he had done in my life and for revealing himself to me. I thanked him also for Yeshua who by his death according to the biblical prophecies had saved me and forgiven my sins. I submitted my life to him and asked him to guide me and to use me.

These were tremendous changes in my life. I had discovered the God of Israel in the Messiah Yeshua. Everything had changed. Now I saw meaning and order in all around me. Everything had a reason and there was a goal to life. The Tenach and the New Testament, which had been a sealed book to me, now became alive and revealed God and his will and truth. My whole philosophy of life, my beliefs concerning life and death, morals and faith had been drastically changed.

I remained in Europe for several more months. As the date of my return home drew near I wrote to my parents and told them something of what had happened to me. When I got back home there was a period of suspicion and of criticism, but they slowly realised that I had changed for the better, and my relationship to my parents has steadily improved ever since.

# 5

# Shaul—Dreams and Visions

*I was born in 1951* in a tent by the seashore in a transition camp near the town of Hadera in Israel. My parents had emigrated from Iraq to Israel that same year. The young state was poor and had to absorb hundreds of thousands of destitute Jewish refugees from Arab lands.

Although we were not blessed with material possessions, we had a happy childhood. There were six brothers and sisters in the family. We grew up with lots of love and warmth and our parents always had time for us.

For the adults it was a difficult time, as they adapted to a new country and struggled to make ends meet. For us as children it was fun. The blue Mediterranean with its white sandy beaches was very near. We spent many happy hours swimming, fishing and playing on the beach. Around our camp were many trees and bushes and behind them stretched the open fields. It was a wonderful place for outdoor fun and games. We would play hide and seek, cowboys and Indians and other childhood games. We saw wild rabbits, jackals and foxes as well as snakes and scorpions. It was wonderful living so close to nature. At night we could see the stars as we lay in the tent, or in winter, hear the sound of the rain as it drummed on the canvas.

My parents were quite religious. I was first sent to a religious kindergarten and then to a religious primary school. As a little child I would accompany my parents to the synagogue. I loved the place. Often after nursery or school hours I would go alone to the synagogue, a distance of almost half a mile from our home. My parents knew that if I wasn't around they could find me there. I loved watching the older men return from their day's work, wash their feet and enter the synagogue. They would munch on a piece of fruit and then settle down to learned discussions on our religious laws and traditions, on the rebirth of Israel— and on the Messiah.

I always loved hearing about the Messiah. I longed for his appearing. I used to dream about him at night; he always held a special attraction for me.

As far back as I can remember, I always knew deep down in my heart that God is my father. He never seemed to be a stranger or far away from me, he was always close by me. I remember sometimes sitting on a stone outside our tent at night, looking up into the sky and talking to my heavenly father. I knew that he heard me and that he cared for me.

As a child, I used to dream a lot—I still do. I dreamt about the coming of the Messiah and about the events of the last days.

At the school I attended we had religious instruction in addition to the secular subjects. We would read the Tenach and study the various commentaries of our sages on the passages we had read. At first I had a Children's Picture Bible, but as soon as I could read well I was given a real Tenach with the Targum of Onkelos on one side of the sacred text and Rashi's commentary on the other. I loved the Bible stories and spent much time reading through them. I especially admired Moses whose figure dominates the first five books. He seemed very impressive to me and I imagined the Messiah would be similar to him.

At home we always kept the kashrut laws and the Sabbath and we celebrated all the feasts of Israel. I was an uncomplicated, naive religious boy, and I accepted all I was taught and drank in all the details about God and the Messiah.

As I grew older, I noticed a discrepancy between institutional religion and the simple faith in God I had observed in the Tenach. I saw well-known teachers behaving contrary to the laws they themselves taught us were God's laws as given in the Tenach. It was a disappointment for me to realise that religion was no longer what God had intended it to be. The hypocrisy offended me. This wasn't the religion God had commanded us at Sinai.

When I was twelve I decided that I did not want to go on to a religious high school (Yeshiva) as my parents expected me to. I removed the kippah from my head and joined a secular kibbutz nearby. There I was confronted with a secular and permissive society. Deep down I always kept alive the knowledge that God was my father and that I would be privileged to witness the appearance of the Messiah, the son of David. I was sure I would live to serve him.

On my arrival at the kibbutz I was a very thin and lanky chap. The other boys laughed at me and nicknamed me 'Narrow Shoulders'. That hurt! In the narrow and confined world of a kibbutz it is easy to get a stigma attached to you but almost impossible ever to get rid of it. I envied the other boys who all seemed so well-built and strong. My brother suggested I do something about it and start some fitness exercises. I gladly accepted his advice, and would daily spend an hour or two lifting weights and practising judo and other sports.

The change was dramatic. Within a short time I was completely different. My body became broad-shouldered and massive. I looked like a real Rambo and they didn't dare laugh at me any more. But inside I remained the same. I wasn't violent and I retained my childish faith in God.

The kibbutz taught us positive values of communal life, Zionism and a willingness to sacrifice. We were taught to give our best to society and to the state. So when I reached army age I volunteered to join the paratroopers where I served for three years.

One day during my army service I had to go to Tel-Aviv in order to catch a special transport to the Sinai. Whilst walking around the Tel-Aviv central bus station, I happened to look up to the sky and was transfixed with amazement. Right there across the sky I saw the name 'YESHUA' clearly written in huge flaming letters. Although I had never heard the name before, I realised at once that it must be the Messiah's own name.

In the kibbutz I had met volunteers from abroad and had chatted with them. They never spoke to me about their religion. I knew I was Jewish, a member of the chosen people, and that it was forbidden for us to intermingle with the Gentiles. I wasn't interested in Gentile religions.

Shortly after finishing my army service I met Zehava on the kibbutz. She was dark and pretty and the very first time we met I knew that she would be my wife! She laughed when I later told her of that first impression. We became friendly and some time later decided to be married. Right at the start of our relationship I told her that although I loved her very much and wanted to be with her for ever, I was expecting the coming of the Messiah, and might have to leave her to join his service when he appeared.

Zehava had always attended secular schools where the teachers claimed that God did not exist and that the Bible was a compilation of myths and legends. However, at that time she was searching for God and wanted to know more about him.

We were married in 1973 whilst still kibbutz members. I worked at various jobs—in the orchard and in the dairy farm. Some years later we left the kibbutz and moved to Rosh-Pinah in Galilee.

I had always loved reading the Tenach. I especially enjoyed reading the historical books. For some reason, whenever I got to the prophets—from Isaiah onwards—I would notice a strange heaviness, as though a heavy veil pressed on my eyelids. I would read—but I couldn't understand; my eyes were heavy and I would fall asleep.

I was always dreaming of the last days and of the coming of the Messiah. One night I dreamt that I heard a voice speaking to me from heaven. It was strong and authoritative and I knew it was God's voice. He said: 'Soon your Lord will appear. When you see him run towards him, bow down and say: Speak, Lord, your servant hears.' I found myself standing in a desert, filthy from the sand and the sweat. I thought: 'Oh no! These are the very words Samuel used when God appeared to him. This means that I am about to see God himself. If I see him I will die.' I also remembered Abraham who had run towards the three angels one of whom was God himself.

Suddenly, some yards above me in the desert sky three forms appeared. I realised that the two outer ones were angels—I could only see their beautiful faces, their hands and their feet. Of the central figure I could see the bearded face with a white cap on his head. His body was covered by a white robe lined with gold that reached down to his feet.

His arms were crossed against his breast. I immediately thought of the high priest and his garments as described in the Tenach. The figures descended to the desert sand. I ran towards the central figure, knelt before him and said: 'Speak, for your servant hears.' I was afraid to say 'Lord'. I looked into his face and thought: 'If I die I have at least seen God.'

He started to speak, and the words came flaming out of his mouth and arranged themselves in lines. I couldn't understand the words, but I felt that he was cleansing and purifying me in the innermost depths of my being. I knew that this must be the Messiah.

The figures then went up and disappeared into the desert sky. I found myself all alone in the desert, but completely clean and pure. Then I awoke.

We were living in Rosh-Pinah at that time. Shortly after this vision I was speaking to a friend of mine, Dov, who was unemployed. I wanted to try and help him find a job. 'Don't worry, Shaul,' he said, 'God will help me.' 'Since when were you that intimate with God?' I asked. He answered: 'I am a messianic Jew and believe that Yeshua is the Messiah.'

When he uttered the name 'Yeshua' I felt something stir within me. I had never forgotten the vision I had had at the Tel-Aviv central bus station during my military service, when I had seen this name 'Yeshua' clearly written across the sky. I invited Dov and his wife to visit us and to chat with us about the Messiah.

Whilst living on the kibbutz, I had noticed that they received free Bibles every now and then to give to their pupils in the school. These Bibles included the New Testament, and they would always tear out the New Testament part before giving us the Bibles. Somehow I had managed to obtain one of these torn-out New Testaments and had

kept it all these years. We still had it in our home though I
had never looked at it before. Now, after my conversation
with Dov, my curiosity was aroused.

I used to have a bad habit of going to the rest-room with
a cigarette, a cup of coffee and a newspaper. That day I
took the torn New Testament instead and started reading
it. I couldn't stop. I read and read till I reached the Gospel
of John. I said to myself: 'Yes, this is the very same person I
saw in my dream, this is the same Yeshua whose name I
saw written in flaming letters across the Tel-Aviv sky, this
is the Messiah!'

Dov and his wife visited us and we sat and talked about
the Messiah. Finally I said: 'See, Dov, maybe I am crazy
and maybe you are crazy too. But I must know if there are
others as crazy as us around this place before I can commit
myself. I know that Yeshua is the Messiah, I have seen him,
but I want to be sure that there are other Jews here who
believe in him.' To my surprise there appeared to be other
Jews in Rosh Pinah who believed in Yeshua. That very
evening Dov took me to meet them and I saw them with
my own eyes—Reuben, Benjamin, Sharon, Shmuel and
others. I was overjoyed to realise that I wasn't the only
crazy Jew in town! I was so happy to see them and say to
them: 'I believe as you do. I am happy to have discovered
brothers and sisters in the faith.'

Zehava came to faith in the Messiah a fortnight later. I
didn't put any pressure on her, it was her own independent
decision born of a deep inner conviction.

I believed in Yeshua as the Messiah, not because some
person had convinced me of his claims, but because all my
life I had wanted to know God better and all my life I had
sought for the Messiah. God heard my pleas and in his
mercy revealed Yeshua to me as the Messiah of Israel by
means of these dreams and visions.

I want to challenge any Israeli reading this book to turn to God and sincerely say: 'God, I don't know how to approach you, but as a Jew I want to know you and the Messiah you have promised us. Please reveal yourself to me.'

Since I came to know Yeshua, I am a completed Jew. I belong to the true Judaism—not the Judaism of the Middle Ages, of external rites and traditions. Yeshua sets us free. Free from the fear of the judgement, free to love others, free from hatred, jealousy and fanaticism. Now I am more Jewish than ever before and more faithful to my people. I want to lead an honest life, pay my taxes as they are due, be a good citizen and love and serve my people.

The veil that kept me from understanding the prophets has been removed. Zehava and I were astounded when reading the Tenach to find the Messiah on every page. We understood that God had intended Israel to be a light to the Gentiles through the Messiah. We realised that Isaiah's words in chapter 29 (verses 10-13) about the sealed book had been fulfilled. Our sages and rabbis read the Scriptures and don't realise that they speak of Yeshua. They spend their time discussing religious regulations, compiling commentaries, but can't see the great light of the Messiah revealed in the book.

In Yeshua the veil has been removed. The book is open and easily understood. From Genesis to Revelation we discovered the Messiah in his two roles. First as the sacrifice for our sins, the suffering Servant of God who gives redemption and forgiveness, and secondly as the King Messiah who is yet to return to his people and set up his kingdom of righteousness.

We moved from Rosh Pinah to Tiberias, and our congregation in Tiberias has passed through some difficult times. We have been harassed and attacked and some of our equipment has been destroyed. Yet God gave me and the others involved a spirit of restraint and of forgiveness in these times of crisis.

In Tiberias we had a well-known tough guy nicknamed 'the red demon'. He was a dangerous fellow who had recently become a 'penitent' and turned religious. One day as I was driving home from the market, I felt God telling me to turn back and meet this fellow whose real name was Yitzhak Cohen. I returned to the market and got out of the car. Suddenly I heard a voice calling 'Shaul, Shaul.' It was Yitzhak without his beard and side curls. He had left the orthodox camp. He embraced me and said: 'You messianic Jews are true believers. All the orthodox Jews here, including Yad Leachim, know it and even admire you for it.' He invited me to a boat ride with him on the lake and we could talk about Yeshua.

Religion is a substitute for a living faith. When I don't hear God's voice speaking to me any more, I create religious formulas. This happens in all religions, Judaism, Christianity and Islam. The real solution is the Messiah himself living in us and changing us from within, creating us anew, cleansing and forgiving us. Through him we have a personal relationship with God which is the most important thing in our lives.

I am sad that some of our orthodox friends hate us. I love them. They are a part of our nation. Many of them sincerely seek God's presence and will, but as it is written: 'Hardness of heart has partially happened to them until the fulness of the Gentiles has come in.' May God grant that this fulness will soon be attained!

When my parents first heard that I believed in Yeshua, they were convinced that I was in financial difficulties and that I was cleverly trying to get money out of the so-called 'mission'—that mysterious and frightening institution that kidnaps pure souls by tempting and bribing them with money! (That is a typical Jewish view of Christian work in Israel, often blindly accepted as the truth by the media and the masses.)

My father once said to me: 'Shaul, you must be in serious financial difficulties for you to turn to the Christians.' 'Not on your life,' I answered, 'What is Christianity?' 'Oh,' he said, 'it is those who believe in Yeshu as you now do.' 'Dad,' I answered, 'I don't believe in a Yeshu, I believe in Yeshua the Son of David.' I went on to explain to him a few truths from the Tenach. He listened, then persisted: 'But what of the mission? Don't you know that they distribute money?'

'No Dad,' I answered, 'since I believed most of my old friends have dropped me, many jobs have been shut to me, and it is a struggle to make ends meet. But you can't buy faith with money, it is a free gift of God.'

He argued with me for a while, then he asked me to prove my faith to him from the Tenach. I happily spoke to him from Moses and the Prophets. He listened for a while and then said: 'I now see that you sincerely believe in it. But you must decide—either you are my son or you believe in Yeshua, you can't be both.'

'No Dad,' I said, 'I am your son more than ever before. Just look around and see how many children ill-treat their parents. Everywhere you find quarrels between fathers and sons. But because Yeshua lives in my heart I now love and respect you more than ever before. As my earthly father you symbolise my heavenly father.'

For a long time we had difficulties with my parents. They tried various ways to convince us that we were wrong. Finally they gave up, acknowledging that we knew the Scriptures better than they did and that we were sincere in our faith—it wasn't the 'mission'.

Their attitudes towards us gradually improved. Some years later my father said: 'My son, I have noticed that you lead a good life and I enjoy visiting your home and being with your family.'

He also finally understood that I had remained a Jew. His greatest fear all along was that I had turned into a Gentile, thus betraying my people. Dad is now open to Yeshua, and when we pray in Yeshua's name he says 'Amen'.

Of course we try our best not to be a stumbling block to our families or to others. As Jews we keep the Sabbath, we keep kashrut and we celebrate all the biblical feasts. We dwell amongst our people and are part of them.

Zehava's parents always treated us favourably. They had read the New Testament and said: 'Yeshua isn't a Gentile; he is totally Jewish.'

Today I am active as an elder in our congregation, devoting my time and energies to this important ministry.

Zehava is a real helpmeet to me. Through our faith in the Messiah we have learnt to live our family life according to his principles. Sharing and communication are a priority and we respect each other's identity and gifts.

We have eight children for whom we praise God. We bring them up to love Yeshua, but also allow them to observe the world around them. They must develop their own ability to discern between good and evil, not as pre-programmed robots, but as independent human beings created in God's image. Of course they have their problems, and they ask questions about the reason for suffering and misery and war in this world. Together we pray for God's answers to these questions.

My deep and sincere prayer is for God to open the eyes of the nation dwelling in Zion, that the veil may be removed and that spiritual showers of blessing be poured on to our land. I pray for the salvation of Israel.

I still expect to see the Messiah—the one who died for my sins—he himself will soon return!

I believe in the coming of the Messiah, and though he tarry, yet will I believe. I shall patiently await him.

The prophecies are being fulfilled and Jews are returning to their homeland from the far North. The dry bones are putting on sinews, flesh and skin. Come, O Spirit and blow life into these dry bones! Purify our hearts, O Lord of the universe, to serve the Messiah faithfully and with all our hearts!

# 6

# Tali—Yearning for Meaning

*I was born in Jerusalem* in 1963. My father's family came from Egypt. Dad was an only child, born when his father was seventy years old! His father had died when he was thirteen.

My mother's family has lived in Jerusalem for four generations and originally came from Aleppo in Syria. Her mother died when she was nine, and she had to take care of her three younger brothers as she was the eldest child. Her father remarried, and he had another five children.

My parents are not religious, but they believe in God, keep the Jewish feasts and attend synagogue on the Day of Atonement.

We lived in the Jerusalem suburb of Kiryat Yovel. I was the only daughter, with one older brother and two younger. It wasn't easy because my parents always expected more of me as a girl than they did of the boys.

My father was involved in a bad road accident when I was ten years old. He lost an eye and suffered a head injury.

As a result of these injuries he became very nervous and bad-tempered and we all suffered the consequences.

Being the only girl at home, I didn't have anyone I could talk to about the things that really mattered to me, anyone I could share my feelings with. My mother had grown up without her mother and didn't know how to express her feelings and how to relate to me as a girl.

As a result I grew up with unresolved problems, childhood scars that hurt but couldn't be shared with anyone. I kept it all to myself and repressed my woes. As a result I suffered from a lack of self-esteem and confidence and was afraid of what people would think of me.

As a child I just loved reading anything I could lay my hands on—everyone called me a bookworm. I was a constant visitor at the local library, and when I had finished reading all the books in the children's section, they had to allow me to move on to the adult section of the library to satisfy my hunger for books. It was my way of escaping the harsh realities of life. Even in class I would read with the book hidden under the desk.

At school I was a very average pupil. I didn't like sports, but I managed to survive in most subjects. I was always worried about the true meaning of life.. I remember that when I was twelve I wrestled with the question of God's existence. My dog went missing one day so I said to God : 'If you exist, please bring her back and I will believe in you.' Nothing happened so I decided that there was no God.

As a teenager in high school I was still bothered by the quest for meaning in life. Here is a poem I wrote when I was seventeen which expressed my feelings of despair at that time.

Is there someone up there who can really help,
someone I can talk to who will listen to me?
How long must I bear the burden of maturity?
I am slowly breaking, waiting for some hope
that is slow to come to me.
I try to think, maybe I am guilty, wrong,
I have made many mistakes, but for how long
must I be punished? Is there no atonement?
I cry out again and again, please help me!

On graduating from high school when I was eighteen, I
joined the Nachal (pioneer unit) brigade. Forty of us were
sent to Kibbutz Maaleh-Hahamisha near Jerusalem for
eight months of pre-army training. At that time there were
also a number of Finnish volunteers in the kibbutz, and as
we often worked together I became quite friendly with
some of them, especially with a blond blue-eyed girl called
Anya who often worked with me in the kibbutz rest home.
She had a serenity about her that I envied and she was
always very friendly to everyone. I was attracted to her and
we became good friends.

The Finns were considered to be the best workers on the
kibbutz. I noticed they had a peace about them that I
lacked, and was attracted to them. As we chatted they told
me of their faith in Yeshua. At that time I only knew what I
had learnt at school about him: he was a historical figure,
the founder of a new religion like Buddha or Muhammad.
He's all right for the Gentiles, was my attitude, but he is
definitely not for us Jews.

The groups of volunteers came and went, but I kept up
the contact with some of the friends I had made through
correspondence with them after their return to Finland.
Anya was very faithful in writing to me and to every letter
she added a quote from the Bible. I liked her letters but I

didn't like her quotes! It was something that simply held no interest for me.

In our unit we also had some Jewish volunteers from abroad, in addition to the Israelis. After work we would meet in the disco, have a drink in a pub and search for entertainment. I was involved in it all but never really enjoyed these activities and never felt any sense of fulfilment in them.

After the eight-month training period, we joined the regular army and were assigned to man a new settlement point on a hilltop. We were a close knit group and got on well with each other. We learned to do everything together—both work and leisure activities. On the whole I thoroughly enjoyed my army service. I was in charge of the labour division unit, and so I got to know them all well and I learned a lot about human nature.

With the start of the war in Lebanon in 1982, the men were sent to the front and we girls back to the kibbutz until the end of the hostilities. During that war, two boys from my unit were killed in battle and two others were taken prisoner. They were all good friends of mine, and I was terribly shocked. I could not understand how God, if he existed, could allow such disasters to happen. To Anya in Finland I wrote: 'How can you believe in a loving God when you experience such terrible things?'

The army taught me to be independent and to get along in society. We also travelled around a lot and I learned to love the countryside. On my release from the army I remained in the kibbutz for an additional three months.

In honour of my release from army service, my parents offered me the gift of a return flight ticket to India. I was attracted to the mysticism and the mysteriousness of the Far East. It was a popular fashion at that time amongst

Israeli youth to take a trip out there and gather 'experiences'.

India made a powerful impact on my life. On the one hand, everything seemed so colourful and beautiful. On the other hand, I saw the terrible poverty and squalor, the blind faith in idols and in fate and the holy cows eating all they wanted to in the streets whilst human beings died of hunger.

Everything seemed so new and different. Lepers stretched out their hands to me for money and children whose limbs had been deliberately broken begged on the streets. It was attractive and loathsome at the same time.

I tried a little of everything—drugs, mysticism, whatever, but didn't really get involved in them. I met young Israelis there who had joined Ashrams and were learning Yoga in their quest for inner peace. I thoroughly enjoyed the freedom, the cheap prices and the variety, but after two months it was time for me to return home.

The moment I got back home, I decided I wanted to travel again to India. I looked for work that would allow me to save money for the trip and I finally got a job as a cashier in the Hotel Laromme in Jerusalem. I worked hard and saved and looked forward expectantly to the day I could again fly out to the Far East.

One day I had a phone call from a Finnish couple, Heikki and Rita whom I had met on the kibbutz. They wanted me to visit them in Finland and offered to pay my flight expenses. I didn't hesitate but packed my cases and flew off to the far North for a three-month visit.

Finland is a beautiful country with lots of forest and many lakes. Everything is green and fresh. The only problem was the cold—I was there from September to December and it was far too cold for my taste.

After spending some time with my friends Heikki and

Rita they directed me to a communal Christian farm called 'Beit-Carmel' founded by a religious group who loved Israel and prayed for it. It was run on lines similar to a kibbutz.

Before meals, someone would read from the Bible and they would then sing and pray. Sometimes they would organise seminars for Bible study and they also ran Hebrew language courses.

I worked there for a while milking cows and goats and picking apples. All the people there were believers and they seemed very nice. I sensed that they had something that I lacked in my life. I arrived at the conclusion that their faith in Yeshua made the difference, but was still convinced that this kind of faith wasn't for me.

When I left the farm they gave me as parting gift a copy of the Bible—both Old and New Testaments—in Hebrew. I thanked them, but said that I couldn't accept it. The Old Testament was all right but the New Testament wasn't for me. It simply wasn't a book for Jewish people.

After touring around Finland, I returned for a short visit to the farm prior to my return to Israel. They received me again with much love and kindness. When I finally bade them farewell, they again presented me with the Bible. This time they had all signed their names on the front page, and I couldn't refuse it, so I took it back with me.

I went back home to Jerusalem and lived with my parents. I looked for a job, but couldn't find one. For some reason I didn't feel comfortable any more around my old friends. Their interests were no longer mine. Going around pubs and entertainment spots seemed boring and dull and meaningless.

I was lonely and had little social contact. I had no work and no money. My relationship with my parents deteriorated, especially with my father. It got so bad that I stopped talking to him. This was the worst period in my life.

I was bored and miserable. I had nothing to do with the time that lay heavily on my hands. I then remembered the Bible I had received in Finland, got it out and started reading the New Testament. I read the Gospels. It looked like a good story, but I couldn't see any connection to the Tenach.

In Finland I had also been given a book in Hebrew called *Betrayed*. It deals with a Jewish girl in America who comes to faith in Yeshua as the Messiah of Israel and as the atonement for her sins. Her father desperately tried to prove to her that she was mistaken, but as he studied the Scriptures he himself came to faith in Yeshua.

As I read this book, I clearly saw the prophetic connection of the New Testament to the Tenach. I still remembered the prophets from my studies at high school, and now, after reading the book *Betrayed* I realised there was a distinct probability that Yeshua was the Messiah. He was the only one in Jewish history who had fulfilled many of the messianic prophecies—none of the false Messiahs had done that—so maybe he was the promised Messiah.

I struggled a lot with this question, but couldn't arrive at any clear-cut decision. I prayed to God and said : 'God, if you exist, reveal the answer to me.'

Some time later a Finnish friend visited me and stayed with us for a week. We travelled around the country together, and on the Sabbath she asked me if I would accompany her to the messianic congregation in Jerusalem. I agreed, and so for the first time in my life attended a messianic Jewish service. They sang and prayed and listened to a sermon on the potter and the clay from Jeremiah chapter 18. The speaker emphasised that God could mould us and change us according to his will.

At the end of the service we all went outside and stood around for a while. I suddenly spied a fellow called Shmulik who had been with me at high school. I approached him and said: 'Shmulik, what are you doing here?' I was surprised to hear that he was the speaker's son. We chatted for a while and he invited me to attend the youth gatherings of their congregation, and also to come and see him at a children's camp he was involved in at the time as a leader.

That visit to the congregation showed me that there were Israelis who believed in Yeshua. I decided to go to the camp and meet the young Israelis who were acting as leaders there. When I got there, I was happy to see they were my age and I felt at ease with them. I chatted for a while with a girl called Shira. She asked me if I believed in Yeshua. I answered that I was still struggling with this question, but would like to. Shira suggested we go into a side room where I could pray to accept Yeshua into my life.

We went into the room and she read a verse out of Revelation, chapter 3 verse 20: 'Here I am! I stand at the door and knock. If anyone hears my voice and opens the door, I will come in...' I understood that this was Yeshua standing at the door of my heart, asking to be let in.

I did not know what to say, but Shira guided me in a prayer, and I repeated the words after her. I did not feel anything special, but I knew that this was a turning point in my life, and that from now on my life would be different— I had taken a step from which there was no return.

The change wasn't dramatic. I understood that Yeshua had died for my sins, and that it was the merit of his sacrifice that obtained my forgiveness. I felt a change in my attitude to my parents, and I started talking to my Dad again. I regularly attended services at the congregation, even though at the beginning I didn't always understand all the sermons.

It was only after a year that I found the courage to tell my parents of my new faith. I was afraid of their reaction, afraid they would get angry and not understand me. It was a big shock for them and for some time they wouldn't even talk about it. I learned that God stands by my side in difficult situations and he helped me through it all. I also learned that I could turn to him and share with him all the problems of my life. Gradually their attitudes towards me and my faith improved and I know that they really want the best for me.

Five years had passed between the time when I had first heard the good news when I was eighteen and until I received Yeshua by faith when I was twenty-three years old. During these five years God had been working in my life, changing me and preparing me for this moment. God works at his own pace. He answered the prayers of my friends who had interceded for me for many years.

Today I am working in the Caspari centre in Jerusalem. I have a new family—believing friends with whom I can share all my problems. The main thing in my life is knowing God through Yeshua my Messiah. This is a treasure more valuable to me than anything else in the world.

I love my people and my land, and my prayer is that all Israel might be saved—as predicted in the Scriptures.

# 7

# Yaakov*—A Marine Finds the Way

*My parents were* both born in Romania. As children they were put into concentration camps by the Nazis and there they saw their parents and many members of their families being killed. Somehow they survived the holocaust but were deeply scarred by the terrible experience.

After the Second World War, my father tried to emigrate illegally to Israel but was captured by the British and sent to Cyprus. In 1947 some children were allowed to leave the camps in Cyprus and go to Israel. My father was sixteen, but as he was small for his age, he could pass as a younger boy and so arrived in Israel just before the War of Independence.

Once in Israel he joined the Irgun—the more extreme Jewish faction fighting for an independent Jewish state. After independence all the various factions were united in the Israeli army and he fought as a soldier in Galilee until the cease-fire agreements between Israel and the Arab states were signed.

*Yaakov's name has been changed in this book for security reasons.

He met my mother whilst still in the army. After the war they joined a group of young people who tried to set up a new co-operative settlement in central Israel. This project however failed, and after getting married in 1952 they settled in a small moshav near the town of Kfar-Saba, five miles from the then Jordanian border. It was Israel's narrowest point, only ten miles between the Mediterranean and the border.

I was born in 1955. My father was working as a welder, and he became the head of the maintenance shop at a boiler factory. It was a tough time in Israel. Every day someone was killed by terrorist attacks, and it was also a tough time economically. Although he worked hard, we couldn't afford much—no fridge, no TV, no telephone. When my mother became pregnant with my younger brother, my father decided it was time to pack up all we had and move to the USA. We had a distant relative in America who was willing to sponsor us, so that took care of the visa problem.

In 1963 we boarded a ship and set sail for the States. It was a great experience for me as a child. Every evening they had a cartoon show for the kids. It was the first time I had seen cartoons and I thoroughly enjoyed it.

We arrived at New York, sailed past the Statue of Liberty and were processed at Ellis Island like so many millions of immigrants before us. It was a difficult adaptation to a new culture. I didn't know a word of English, and I didn't know any American sports. This made for initial feelings of isolation and rejection. However, I quickly learned baseball and basketball and eventually was accepted in the new environment of my American school.

My parents were quite secular. Their experiences in the holocaust had caused them to lose any faith they might have had in God. They became atheists because of what they saw men do to each other, and they found no answer to the question: 'How could God allow it?' Now in the United States, in order to keep our Jewish identity amongst all those Gentiles, we started attending an orthodox synagogue and they also made me attend Hebrew school two or three afternoons a week after public school hours.

I became quite religious with a strong belief in God. I attended synagogue every Saturday and faithfully put on my tefillin and said my prayers every day.

My father first tried to work as a welder, but his health deteriorated and he became a barber and remained one for twenty-five years. Five days a week he worked as a barber and two days a week as a maintenance man. Ten hours a day, seven days a week he kept going, taking no holidays for many years. It was tough making it in a new country, and my mother had to work too in a Jewish delicatessen shop six days a week to help make ends meet.

I was never close to my parents. They were never at home and I was a latchkey kid—carrying the house key with me at all times, coming back to an empty home and taking care of myself. When my parents finally got home, they were very tired and had no energy left for us children and no patience to listen to what really bothered us.

At school there was a wide mixture of ethnic groups and we all got on quite well together. I picked up English pretty fast, so after the initial difficulties I became a good student—straight A's in all subjects until the seventh grade. I also discovered that the level of mathematics in Israel was much higher than in the American school, and that helped me a lot.

I resented having to go to Hebrew school in the evenings, when the other kids were out playing. At the same time I enjoyed learning Hebrew and stories from the Tenach and something about our ancient history and culture.

By the time I went to high school at sixteen my attitudes had changed. I stopped going to synagogue, and sports took over as the priority in my life. I couldn't have cared less about my studies and stopped doing any homework. I scraped through by passing the tests with good grades. Every day after school I'd be out playing at some sport with my friends—basketball, hockey, football—we had something for every day.

When I graduated from high school I decided to join the marines. I wanted to get away from home and see something different. I was sent to San Diego for basic training. I was in very good physical shape as a result of my involvement in sports, so I didn't find the training too tough, at least not the physical part of it.

The main premise of marine training is that they have to destroy your civilian personality with its thought patterns and habits, and rebuild you in the marine mould—a soldier willing and able to engage in hand-to-hand combat, to kill or be killed.

After basic training I enrolled in the Air Traffic Control School of the Marines Air Wing. On graduation I was assigned to an airfield in Yuma, Arizona, a small town of twelve thousand inhabitants way out in the desert. I had asked to be stationed on the East Coast or near Los Angeles. I was looking forward to the big city life and excitement. Instead I was sent to this out-of-the-way place in the Arizona desert.

Actually, it was quite a good life. As an air traffic controller I had a 6.00am to 2.00pm job, good pay and good accommodation.

I wasn't sent to Vietnam, but because I had served during that time I was classified as a war veteran and the military later helped by paying my college fees. Off duty I would go to movies, drink and gamble with other soldiers in the same situation as me. I quite enjoyed this lifestyle and had no worries in the world.

There was one guy in our unit who was different and rather strange. He used to repair the radios on the planes and he lived two doors down from me. Ben didn't join our crowd, and he would spend hours talking to me about what it was like to be Jewish, and about Israel. I couldn't figure him out. I wondered why this Gentile should care for me, a Jew. Why was he interested in Jewish things? Why was he so different from all the others there?

From my background I knew that Christians hated Jews. It was a fact of life I grew up with. As a child I had listened to my parent's stories of their experiences during the holocaust. It was Christians—church-going, cross-bearing Christians—who had killed my grandparents and six million Jews. The cross was to me a sign of persecution, torture and death.

As a teenager I was taunted in our neighbourhood for being Jewish and even remember my father standing guard with a rifle in our house because some people had threatened to burn it down. All these experiences and impressions taught me very clearly that all Gentiles hate us Jews. You just couldn't trust them. Even when they appeared to be friendly, they might stab you in the back the moment you turned round.

One day in the summer of 1975 Ben invited me to an 'Andrew' dinner he and some of his friends had organised. The idea was that every 'Peter' brought an 'Andrew' with him—I was Ben's 'Andrew'. I was getting rather tired of the party crowd I hung around with, so I gladly agreed to accompany him to this steak dinner. I was surprised to see a large group of people gathered there.

Someone got out a guitar and they started singing. First

they sang some folk songs which I enjoyed. Then they sang a song about God—that went down well with me as I still believed in God. 'These guys are all right,' I thought to myself, 'they believe in God.' After that they sang about Jesus—that wasn't kosher! I'm not one to make waves, so I didn't get up and leave but stayed on and sang along with them. However every time we got to the word 'Jesus' I skipped over it. I couldn't bring my lips to pronounce that name. All I knew about him was that he was the cause of all our troubles. He belonged to the Gentiles. They hated us because of him.

That was the first time I had heard about the biblical faith in Jesus. Naturally, I didn't want to have anything to do with it, but somehow, after that dinner, believers in Jesus suddenly seemed to be everywhere. They seemed to be coming out of the woodwork all over the place. I'd go to the movies, or bowling, or even just hang around the barracks—and I'd bump into them everywhere, always wanting to talk to me about 'him'. I became a professional at saying 'no,' at rejecting all they told me about their faith. I would go over to the attack and leave them tongue-tied as I told them all that Christians had done to our people throughout history.

After three months of this constant barrage, all of a sudden they seemed to disappear again. I stopped running into them.

I was very happy. I thought I had finally got rid of them and didn't have to worry any more about being pestered by these Jesus people.

I went back to my old lifestyle. Cash, Cars and Cuties— these were the three C's I tried to build my life around. I had a good salary from the marines and no expenses for food, lodging and medical care. I bought a fancy car with metal flake paint that glittered in the sun, vinyl top and a high performance engine. I had a girl friend in Arizona and one in Tennessee and another in Ohio. I had everything I thought I wanted — but deep down I wasn't happy. There was a deep void within me that I couldn't fill with any of these things.

Life flowed on in this way for a while, and then things started to go wrong for me. I got heavily into debt through gambling. My far-away girl friends found replacements for me nearer at hand and decided to jilt me. Then one night in December 1975 while driving my Arizona girl friend home through the desert, the car suddenly skidded and went off the road. It flew down the six-foot embankment and landed on the lower desert level where it crashed into a telephone pole.

My girl friend was shoved under the instrument panel and received injuries all over her body. Although I had not belted up, I was miraculously not thrown through the windscreen and did not seem to have sustained any injuries. I quickly administered first-aid to my friend and then clambered up the embankment back to the road to try and flag down some car and get her to the nearest hospital. It was eleven at night and no vehicle would stop. I turned back to return to my car when suddenly I saw that someone had parked his motor-home for the night a hundred yards from where I stood. I ran and woke the guy up and together we transported my girl friend to hospital.

She soon recovered from her injuries, but our relationship was terminated. My car was a total loss and not worth repairing.

This accident shook me up a lot. I realised that God was trying to get a message through to me, that he was saying that something was wrong in my life.

I had now lost my car, my money and my last girl friend. Why had God saved me? What did he want of me? I decided I would try to please him the only way I knew: by going back to being an observant Jew.

Having lost everything I was interested in, I began to feel rather depressed and sorry for myself. One day in January 1976 I saw Ben sitting alone in the dining hall. I sat down next to him and told him my sad story. He listened sympathetically then said: 'Jesus can give you a new life.' I knew Jesus wasn't for me, so I said I'd think about it.

Two days later the same thing happened. I went to the Chow Hall to get some food and saw Ben sitting there all by himself. I sat down beside him and told him my sad story all over again. He listened again attentively, then he showed me a verse in John chapter 10, verse 10: 'The thief comes only to steal and kill and destroy; I have come that they may have life, and have it to the full.' At that time I had no interest whatsoever in heaven, eternal life and similar things believers talked about. This verse showed me for the first time that Jesus could give me a new life right here on this earth—not just in the sweet bye and bye, but in the nasty now!

I was getting so tired with my old life that I thought: 'Well, maybe there is something there.' Ben then shared another verse with me, from Romans chapter 1, verse 16: 'I am not ashamed of the gospel, because it is the power of God for the salvation of everyone who believes; first for the Jew, then for the Gentile.' When I read the words 'first for the Jew' my eyes were suddenly opened. The blindness was removed and I realised that Jesus was for the Jews. I said: 'OK, I'm willing to put my trust in him.' All I grasped at that point was that he had died for my sins and that he was the answer. I realised that I was a sinner, separated from God, and that through Jesus I could now find the way back to him. The day was January the 15th.

Ben invited me to come later and see him again in his

room. I went for a while to my own room and sat at my desk struggling with the issue: yes—no, yes—no. But God convinced me that Jesus was the answer. At three o'clock that afternoon I knocked at Ben's door, and there in his room I asked Jesus to come into my life.

I thought that I could just try it out for a while and if it didn't help I could leave it alone. I didn't realise that he would come into my life and take over, but that's what happened!

Next day I was conscious of the fact that I felt differently and thought differently. Jesus gave me real power and victory over sin, and I was overjoyed.

It took three months before I was able to enter a church. It took over a year to feel comfortable pronouncing the name of Jesus. But God broke these barriers down and helped me grow and mature in the faith. Three months after I had come to faith I realised that I must make the Lord the first priority in my life and I committed myself to walk in his ways. At that point I broke off all the entanglements I still had with the world, and I served the last two and a half years of my time in the marines as a committed believer in Jesus.

It was exciting. In the service all your needs are taken care of, so you can spend all your free time serving God. You have loads of time on your hands, so you can read your Bible, have fellowship and witness without undue pressure and without the entanglements of civilian life.

About a year and a half after I became a believer, a team from 'Jews for Jesus' came to sing in Yuma, and that was the first time I had met other Jewish believers. It was great to see that there were other Jews like me who believed that Jesus was the Messiah. It was also wonderful to realise that we could remain faithful to our Jewish identity and culture, having come back to our Jewish Messiah Yeshua.

After leaving the marines, I spent a year in Ohio working as a supervisor with United Processor Services. In the summer I went back to Arizona for a training programme, and whilst there God called me to full-time service—first to train at Moody Bible Institute in Chicago and then to return to Israel to serve him there. It was a very clear call and I obeyed as best I could. I enrolled in Moody, and as I had to work to make ends meet, it took me five years to finish the course. I worked full-time as a computer operator for a bus company whilst studying, and finally graduated with honours in 1989.

The same summer that God called me to full-time service, he also spoke to me about my future wife. He spoke to me about a girl in my home congregation that he was preparing for me. I had committed myself never to date again, but to trust the Lord for my life partner. He worked it all out and eventually brought us together and united in his service.

After I came to faith in Jesus, it took me a year and a half to pluck up courage to tell my parents about it. One day when I was back home for a visit I went out for a walk with Dad and then told him that I had become a believer in Jesus. He burst out into a prolonged and hysterical fit of laughter. He just couldn't believe that I had joined the people who had killed his father and caused so much suffering for the Jewish people—that was how he saw it! It actually took him eleven years to come to terms with it.

My parents first thought it was just the marine corps that had brain-washed me into wanting to be like everybody else, into believing I had a secure place in heaven so I would be ready to die on the front lines. They thought that once I got back into civilian life I would return to my old ways.

When that didn't happen, and when instead of that my brother also came to the same faith in Jesus, they were really upset and turned me out of their house. Several months later they allowed me to visit them occasionally on condition that I stayed away from my younger brother. After a couple of years, things improved slightly, but it was my marriage that finally brought reconciliation, and when our first son—their first grandson—was born, that really turned things around for us and we now have a very good relationship with them.

Finally we were ready to return to Israel and start a new life there. Although I had spent twenty-seven years in the States, I had never forgotten my Israeli roots and immediately felt very much at home here. I found work as a computer operator and programmer, and am happy to be where God wants me to be. I have a great love for my people and for the land itself. As a completed Jew, I count it a privilege to belong to Abraham's seed and to the Messiah's own people. It is not that we are any better—but it is very special to know that you belong to the nation of the patriarchs, the prophets, the Messiah and the apostles. Knowing my heritage and culture, I long for my own people to come to know the Jewish God personally through faith in the Jewish Messiah.

Keeping all the traditions and commandments can make you proud as you claim merit with God for what you are doing. It needs humility to acknowledge that you are a sinner who cannot make his own way to heaven, but needs to trust in Yeshua the Jewish Messiah, who gave his life as an atonement for your sins and thus reconciled you to God. Pride is a great stumbling block in our way to God. Humility and faith in the Messiah open the way to a personal relationship with the God of our fathers. This is the only way to have our sins forgiven and to receive peace with God.

I thank God for opening my eyes to this truth, and I

# 8

# Batyah—Typesetting a Strange Book

*My parents came* to the land of Israel in 1938 from Yemen. They were both young and single at that time. They met and got to know each other here in Israel, and it was in Jerusalem that they got married, settled down and raised their family.

The economic situation was very bad at that time. My father had to work very hard laying tiles in the building trade. My mother also had to find outside employment in order to help the family income.

Like all Yemenite Jews, my parents were faithful to their religion and traditions. They kept the commandments and loved the Torah. My father daily read the Tenach and daily attended synagogue.

I was born in Jerusalem in 1955 as the youngest child in our family, following two brothers and two sisters. Being the youngest they all spoiled me. I had a happy childhood and experienced a lot of love and warmth in my family— even now I look back with longing to my childhood days.

In the Yemenite community everything was done

together by all the families in the neighbourhood. We would laugh together and weep together and all would pool together to help anyone in need. It was very beautiful and touching.

As a child I loved animals and always longed for a dog of my own. When I was ten years old we found a stray dog in the street whom we took home and adopted. We called him Amitz (meaning bold). He was a mongrel, but very handsome with white fur and black spots. I really loved him. Every day when I returned home from school he would run to meet me, joyfully wagging his tail.

After living with us for two years he was run over one day by a car in the street near our house. This was a terrible shock to me, my most traumatic experience as a child. I felt I had lost someone very near and dear who would never return. We had a funeral service for Amitz. The neighbours all attended and we buried him in our yard and even set him a gravestone.

I attended a religious elementary school, where I enjoyed literature, Bible and arts and crafts. From the age of ten I was asked to read children's stories on the radio. That was very interesting and exciting.

Our neighbours had a cousin who often visited them as his own parents were divorced. I was then twelve years old, and he seemed to be a very handsome fellow. We became good friends, but my mother didn't agree to anyone dating me at that young age. He also came from a Moroccan family and was very secular, whilst we were Yemenite and religious—my parents didn't allow this relationship to develop any further.

I finished primary school at thirteen, and I decided that I wanted to continue my schooling at a secular high school. At that age I started to feel a rebelliousness stirring within me against my parents and all they stood for, especially their religion and traditions. It was part of my growing-up process, and although I loved my parents and the old customs, I didn't feel that these traditions offered me any fulfilment or that keeping the commandments brought me near to God.

It was the period immediately following the Six Day War, when Jerusalem was reunited and we experienced the fulfilment of many prophecies. These events had a great impact on me and aroused in me many questions about God, about the Tenach, about death and about eternal life.

The secular school I now attended was no place to look for answers to these questions. Although I had decided to change to this school of my own free will, the transition was something of a shock to me. Our Bible teacher was a convinced atheist and treated the few religious pupils in our class with a marked cynicism. I tried to adapt to the secular environment, but my faith in God lived on and I realised how superficial and empty this liberal and permissive world I now lived in really was.

I graduated from high school and was called up for military service in the navy when I was eighteen. I was still very rebellious towards religion and tradition and tried to fill my life with new meaning by entertainment and romantic adventures.

At my brother's wedding I met a fellow called Danny who was the photographer. He was the brother of my sister's best friend. We dated and this successful photographer wooed me all through my military service. I was very naive and dreamt that marriage would be the solution to all my problems. I was sure marriage would be fun, giving me independence from my parents and my own home. I agreed to marry him, and immediately on my release from the army when I was only nineteen we got married.

Even now I can't understand why I agreed to marry him.

My parents advised me to end the relationship, but I wouldn't listen to them. I was still very rebellious, and I was also very stubborn. I realised the gap between us—he came from a totally different background to mine. He was a convinced atheist and very materialistic. However, I felt sure that within the marriage framework we would be able to solve all our problems and bridge all the gaps. I went my own way and did what I felt like doing—and have since paid dearly for it over many years.

Once we were married our life together was so difficult that we started thinking of divorce after only six months. A good friend who was a Rabbi counselled us, hoping to save our marriage and to help us rebuild our relationship, but it was to no avail. He finally gave up and advised us to get a divorce.

One and a half years after our wedding, on the very day on which we were to get a divorce, Danny had a terrible accident. He was driving back from Tiberias with a friend when their car went off the road and down a steep slope. The friend was killed on the spot and Danny suffered severe injuries. He had concussion and his thigh bone was broken. He had to lie in plaster for a long time.

This was a hard blow for me. I didn't understand what was happening and I didn't know what to do. Was God trying to tell me something through this accident? Should I remain with Danny? Did I need to change? I remember standing under the shower that day and starting to cry. I said to God: 'I know you exist, show me the reason for this accident and show me what to do.'

I finally decided to stay with Danny and help with his rehabilitation. A week later I discovered that I was pregnant—this was a miracle. Danny's brother visited us and tried to convince me that I should have an abortion. How could I manage with a baby under these conditions, with a severely injured husband who needed all my attention?

I didn't agree with him. I decided that I would keep the baby at any cost. I told him that abortion was against my principles and completely out of the question.

From the beginning of my pregnancy I felt a special blessing and grace of God on my life. Nine months later I gave birth to a wonderful baby girl whom we called Meirav. She completely changed my life, and I felt that God's hand was on me for good.

The period of time following the accident was very tough for me. Danny lay in bed encased in plaster for five months. I did everything for him and he gradually got better, but his attitude to me didn't improve.

At that time I had a part-time job at the Ministry of Finance in Jerusalem. A colleague at work who knew of the crisis in my marriage suggested I join her in a transcendental meditation course. She was sure it would help me in my difficult situation and explained that it was simply a relaxation technique.

I knew nothing about meditation, but I agreed to give it a try as I certainly needed some help. I attended a trial session where they gave us an introduction to the course and I then decided to join. I faithfully attended all sessions, and at the end of the course we had a dedication service at which we were asked to appear with an apple and a clean white handkerchief.

During the ceremony they took us into a room where a large picture of the Maharishi Mahesh Yogi hung on a wall and beneath it they had placed flowers and incense. All of a sudden I realised that this was a pagan religious ceremony—not an innocent technique for self-improvement! I really felt sick. I don't know why I didn't get up and leave the place. For some reason I stayed there till the end of the

ceremony and didn't say a thing. I even continued meditation exercises on my own for another year and a half. I
didn't feel that it helped me, but I was desperate and needed
an escape from my problems.

Some time after that I heard of a printing press in
Jerusalem that was looking for a part-time keyboard operator. I really needed some extra income and so I went for an
interview to the Yanetz printing press in the Talpiot indus-
trial area. They were very nice to me and at the end of the
interview I was told that I had been accepted for the job.
During my first few weeks on the job they taught me to
operate the computer typesetter that prepares the material
for the printing machine.

I prepared various texts for typesetting, and then one
day they brought me a manuscript of the Brit Hadashah
(the New Testament) in a modern, easy-to-understand
Hebrew translation. I got a real shock when I realised what
book it was. 'Oh dear!' I said to myself, 'This book is
hostile to my religion, I can't work on it.' I went through a
time of intense internal turmoil—should I agree to do the
typesetting for this book or should I resign? After much
hesitation I decided that as I really needed this extra job I
had no option but to work on the manuscript.

I did the typesetting for this book, and at the same time I
read it for the first time in my life. I was astounded at what
I found there. I discovered that Yeshua was a Jew, that all
his disciples had been Jews, and that the whole book was
actually full of Jews! This fact completely revolutionised
my approach to the New Testament and to Yeshua.

I read Yeshua's teaching in the Gospels and his words
touched my heart. Here were the answers to so many of the
questions that had bothered me for many years. I finally
arrived at the threshold of an important decision: was
Yeshua really the Messiah of Israel according to the proph-

ecies of the Tenach? I knew that my relationships with family and friends lay in the balance—but I had to make that decision!

I went through a period of several months of internal conflict while I finished the typesetting of the Brit Hadashah and of several messianic books such as *The Hiding Place* and *Joni*. I spoke to believers at work, I read history books and even went to talk to rabbis about it. I searched desperately for the right answer to this question and gradually I arrived at the conclusion that Yeshua really was the Messiah.

Deep down within me I knew this was the truth, but I was still too stubborn to admit it to myself or to others.

One night I lay awake totally confused as I thought over the various aspects of this dilemma. I finally cried out to God: 'I do believe in you, and I believe that you care for me. Please show me whether Yeshua is really the Messiah, please give me a sign!'

That same night I had a dream. I saw an old man with a white beard and white garments. The next day I went to work as usual. On my way back from work I waited at a bus station. Whilst standing there waiting for the bus I suddenly saw that same man I had seen in my dream! He had the same white beard and was dressed all in white. He stood there for some minutes and then disappeared from my view. I now knew that God had answered my prayers and had given me a clear sign.

It was an extraordinary experience and I knew I couldn't refuse him any more. Yeshua is indeed the Messiah, he is the way. I boarded the bus in ecstasy under the powerful impact of that experience. Right there on the spot I surrendered and received Yeshua into my life and I immediately felt waves of God's love and grace flow over me. I also saw myself in a new light as a sinner who needed his cleansing and forgiveness, and I realised that Yeshua is the only way to God and to the atonement he has provided. This was the turning point in my life.

When I arrived back home I immediately told Danny what had happened to me. He wasn't impressed. He had no faith in the supernatural and was sure I was cracking up. Worse than that, he went to his parents and told them the story in a cynical way. 'You know,' he told them, 'Batyah believes in God and is now seeing angels and such like!' They were all complete atheists, and so of course joined in his attitude of mockery and contempt towards me.

My own family on the other hand responded with love and tolerance. They did not embarrass me in any way, as they presumed that if I had arrived at some queer faith it must be the result of my unbearable life with Danny. They still blamed themselves for their failure to dissuade me from marrying him and for the resulting sad state of my life.

Danny's attitude got worse, and he even became violent. He warned me not to invite any believers like me to our home. He was sure I had converted to Christianity and forbade me any contact with other believers. He became more and more suspicious, and finally he applied to a rabbinical court for a divorce, and claimed our daughter for himself on the grounds that I had become a Christian and couldn't bring her up as a Jewess.

The legal process was long and painful, but God answered my prayers and we finally got the divorce. The court decided in my favour and gave me custody of Meirav. That was a happy day for us. I lost all my material goods and had to leave the flat and move in with my parents, but I felt a tremendous sense of relief and I thanked God for all he had done.

During all that time I continued reading in the Tenach and the Brit Hadashah and found much comfort and encouragement in the Scriptures. I also grew in the faith and learnt to trust God more and more as I saw him deal with the little details of my life.

It was a very special time for me in which the chaos of my former life gave way to a new order and frame of reference. The day I gave my life to Yeshua was the happiest day of my life! I opened a new page and felt a deep contentment and a burden to tell all my friends about it.

I had finally found what I had always searched and longed for. I understood that Yeshua by his grace had atoned for my sin and purified me and shed his light on my life. I spent much time in reading the Scriptures, and some verses seemed to leap out of the pages and touch my heart in a special way as they expressed my own feelings at the time. I even composed tunes to several of these verses as God gave me the melodies for them: 'I will greatly rejoice in the Lord.' 'Behold I will trust in the Lord and not be afraid.' 'The Lord is my strength and my song, and he has become my salvation.' These words expressed my exact feelings, and I could identify with the prophets who penned them over two thousand years ago.

Isaiah 53, the forbidden chapter never read in the synagogue, was another portion of Scripture that deeply touched me. I remember the tears rolling down my cheeks when I first read it. '...a man of sorrows, and familiar with suffering...Surely he took up our infirmities and carried our sorrows.' In all of history, only Yeshua fulfilled this prophecy. I understood something of the great mystery of the Messiah suffering as the sacrifice for the sins of his people and for my own sins.

My message today to everyone is that there is hope. We have Messiah now! God is near to us in Messiah—we only need to believe in him and open our hearts to him.

# 9

# Israel Harel—From Death to Life

*Four days before* the end of the school year—I was fifteen and in the tenth grade—I decided that I had had enough of the orderly and hypocritical world that I was living in. I would leave school and parents and go out on my own into the wide world to live as a hippie. I needed to find for myself the true meaning of life and of my existence.

I was convinced that music and drugs were the real answer to the world's ills. I was sick of school, studies and the discipline required there. I wanted to be free and independent and at peace with myself, not bound by traditions or by hypocritical social conventions.

I went to the Tel-Aviv flea market and bought myself an old shabby coat which fitted the image I wanted to convey of myself. I packed a few things in a bag and set out to the north of Israel. Hitching a few rides I finally arrived at my destination, Achziv on the Mediterranean beach south of Nahariya, where that strange fellow Eli Avivi had set up his hippie kingdom.

I first saw the light of day in Kibbutz Hulda where I was born in 1954. Both my parents were 'Sabras', born in Israel. My mother's parents had come from Germany and her father had become one of the leaders of Mapai, the workers' party, and one of the founders of Kibbutz Beit-Hashita. My father's parents had emigrated from Poland and had settled in Haifa where he was born and then moved to the kibbutz where he grew up.

My mother's father died when she was only five years old. She was then brought up by her mother who was a very strict and hard person. Actually both my parents grew up in difficult homes and never experienced a normal and loving family life. This was why they never succeeded in creating for me and for my sister a warm family environment. They made many mistakes and we suffered the results of these mistakes for many years.

When I was three we moved from the kibbutz to the Moshav Sdeh-Moshe in the Lachish region. Here I grew up and spent my childhood years. I attended nursery and first grade in our village, and from the second grade onwards we were all sent to school in neighbouring Kiryat-Gat, the main town for the Lachish region.

A moshav is a small place with a closed society of its own. Everyone knows everything about everyone. It is great to play in the fields and enjoy country life but then everyone pokes his nose into your affairs and if you get stuck with a stigma you never get rid of it.

I have always been rather plump and my friends would often poke fun at me on that account. Having no emotional support at home from my parents I grew up lacking in self-esteem and full of complexes. Because of my shyness I could never hit it off with the girls. I reacted to all of this by behaving in a wild and rebellious manner and became known as the boy who would never behave well either at home or at school.

I was always bothered by many questions such as: Who am I? Why am I here? What is the meaning of life? I couldn't accept the world as it was. I often asked questions that embarrassed my parents and teachers and gave me a reputation for being somewhat crazy amongst my peers.

I saw a lot of hypocrisy at home and in society and I rebelled against it. Our parents would often forbid us things they allowed themselves to do. I couldn't accept that the age difference was a sufficient excuse. My father had a pat answer to all my questions concerning social conventions. 'This is what society has agreed on,' he would say. This never satisfied me and I searched for real answers to my existential questions.

I had an easy life in primary school as I hardly needed to study and I always did well in the exams. I usually had a good report in all subjects—except for conduct. When I moved on to high school I was in for a shock! The requirements were much higher and I did not know how to do serious study. I did not have the patience to sit at home and read and do my homework. As a result I failed the ninth grade and had to do it all over again.

At home I had endless quarrels with my parents. They took me to see a neurologist and later a psychiatrist. They were sure I suffered from epilepsy because I had convulsions when I was angry and frustrated—which was most of the time! Actually a lot of it was put on as I tried to appear as crazy as possible so I wouldn't owe them or the world they represented anything.

Because of my inner conflicts and disappointments at school coupled with bad relationships at home, I decided to register for tenth grade at an agricultural boarding school 'Kannot'. I gladly left home at the start of the new school

year and went to live at the boarding school with other
children my age.

At the new school there were also several kids from the
States who had come for a year of studies in Israel. They
opened up a new world to us by introducing us to contemporary music such as Pink Floyd and Bob Dylan, and also
to the world of drugs. I enthusiastically accepted these new
discoveries. Here were the real answers to all my questions.
Music and drugs were the real solution to all the world's
problems.

This was how I arrived at the decision to leave school
and home and go to Achziv to live as a hippie. I imagined
hippie life to be a wonderful blend of unlimited freedom in
nature's bosom with no social conventions and no strings
attached.

In Achziv I joined a group of youngsters with similar ideas
who had rebelled against normal conventions and believed
hippie life to be the answer to all their quests. We sat
around and smoked hash believing that drugs would open
up a new world to us in which all was love and peace. We
found that drugs would give us a good trip where we would
be happy and good friends with every one. When under the
influence of drugs there seemed to be no demands from the
world and no requirements from anyone. Everything was
fine and everybody was OK. We were sure that this world
of music and drugs would lead us to the ultimate existential
truths.

Our lives took on a certain routine. In summer we
would live in Achziv and sometimes move to Tel-Aviv
where we sauntered around Dizengoff Square and slept in
Meir Park. In winter when the weather turned cold and wet
we would go down to Eilat to enjoy the warmth of the Red
Sea beaches.

Every now and again I would return home to my parents to try and lead a 'normal' life, but it never worked. The old tensions would invariably pop up again and the old wounds which had seemingly healed as a result of the separation would be reopened. It always ended with a violent explosion after which I would leave home and return to my traveller friends. I finally decided that I had had enough of it and left home never to return. I went back to my friends in Achziv and in Eilat, back to the drugs and the music and the leisurely lifestyle.

When the time came for me to be called up to the army I decided that I didn't want to serve. I didn't want to have anything to do with fighting and with wars. After all we firmly believed in world-wide peace and in good will between all nations. Again I did my best to act as if I was crazy and after various examinations I was let off military service.

In 1972 I spent some time in Tel-Aviv with a group of five or six young people. We slept in the parks and in the mornings we would beg for money for our food and drugs. In the evenings we would go to the cinema or would listen to rock concerts. At other times we would just get drunk or high on drugs.

For some reason we then decided to try our luck in Jerusalem and so we moved there. We joined a commune living on the walls of the old city, a random gathering of travellers who came and went at will. We would often sit in the Jaffa Gate enclosure and we sold our blood to the blood bank to get the money we needed for this existence. Being in a group gave us a certain sense of security and strength.

To some extent we were all searching for the truth and didn't want to be satisfied with anything less. We searched and searched and never seemed to find anything. We tried the Guru Mahariji sect then turned to the Children of God and then to the orthodox Diaspora Yeshiva, but all to no avail.

The drug habit soon changed from being a search for new experience and meaning to being a basic necessity I couldn't do without. Gradually I moved from softer to harder drugs, from hash to LSD and on to intravenous injections of heroin. Drugs destroy your will power. I remember a a group of us sitting and discussing for hours and hours who should get up and fetch some water to drink. Nobody wanted to move from his place. It was absurd, but everyone hoped someone else would do the job.

One day as we sat idly in the Jaffa Gate enclosure a woman approached us and asked: 'Have you ever heard about Yeshua?'

I answered that I had but that I didn't want to hear any more. She invited us to her home and offered us some food. We were glad to go with her as it was starting to get cold outside and we were always hungry.

We stayed at her place for a fortnight. Before meals she would always get out her Bible and teach us something from it. She told us that we must be born again and that then God's spirit would enter into our hearts and renew us from within.

She was a somewhat odd character but we put up with her patiently as we enjoyed the warmth in her home and gladly ate all the food set before us.

One day she asked us: 'Well, do you now believe or don't you?' We were scared to say no because we feared that she would throw us out and we had nowhere else to go. After all she provided us with food and her house was warm. So we all said : 'Yes, we do believe.'

Although I didn't really believe, I was astonished at the things she showed us from the Bible. She opened the

Tenach and showed us prophecies about the Messiah which were all seemingly fulfilled by Yeshua in the New Testament. I checked whether her Tenach was the same as our Jewish Tenach, and it was. I started reading it in order to check out her claims. I discovered that there were many prophecies in the Tenach that only one person in history could have fulfilled, and that person was Yeshua of Nazareth.

I now realised that there was some truth in what she had been telling us and became convinced that Yeshua was the promised Messiah. This conclusion sparked off an internal struggle. If he really was the Messiah then I ought to submit my whole being to him, my heart, thoughts, time and money.

Well, I didn't have any money, so that part was easy. I had loads of time on my hands, so that was no problem either. My real problem was that I was not ready to let anyone tell me what to do with myself. I wasn't ready to submit to anyone. I still wanted to be my own boss.

I hesitated and struggled and delayed my decision. Finally like Jonah I ran away from God and kept running away from him for six whole years. I carried a Bible around with me and claimed to be a believer, but I only knew about God; I didn't know him personally.

When I ran away from Yeshua I started to sink ever deeper into the morass of sin and of drugs. Drugs did not give me the same satisfaction as before. I now knew that they were not the answer to life's mysteries. I now knew that only God in Yeshua was the real answer but I didn't want him to rule my life, and as a result I deteriorated and became odd and weird.

I moved back to Tel-Aviv where I would sleep in the city parks. At night I would gather empty bottles which I would then sell in the morning to obtain money for food and drugs. I spent my time in the parks aimlessly looking into space, out of touch with society and cut off from my family and friends who didn't want to know me any more.

In 1974 I travelled to Europe and visited Amsterdam which seemed to be paradise for us travellers. We walked around the parks moving from group to group using and selling drugs. Later I visited Britain and then went on to France where I worked for a while in the grape harvest. When that ended I returned to Amsterdam. It was now autumn, the weather was cold and grey and everyone had disappeared from the parks. My money ran out and when I tried to travel on the train with a stolen ticket I was caught, arrested and deported to Israel with one shekel in my pocket.

On my return to Israel I went to Eilat where I became totally immersed in the drug scene again. Finally I was caught by the police with fifty grams of hash on me and given a date to appear in court. I was on probation for a previous offence and I knew that this time it had to be a prison sentence. But then a miracle took place. First the judge forgot to call my case and later when I was taken to his chamber where the prosecutor demanded the full penalty, the judge merely said: 'Probation for another term and supervision by a probation officer.' It was a real miracle!

My condition however did not improve. On the contrary, I became weirder than ever. The probation officer I had to see regularly suggested that I let myself be admitted to a psychiatric ward but I consistently refused.

I finally despaired of life. I knew that no one cared about me any more, no one wanted me and I had no hope of improvement. I decided to end it all by taking my life. I went into a pharmacy and bought a lot of non-prescription drugs which I intended to swallow. I said to myself that if I died as a result it would be great, but if I survived I would phone my probation officer and ask her to admit me to a psychiatric ward.

I took the medicine and swallowed the lot but I didn't die. Compared to my high intake of drugs these pills must have been relatively weak. So I got in touch with the probation officer who arranged for me to be admitted to the psychiatric hospital in Ashkelon and from there I was moved to the 'Eitanim' psychiatric institute in the Jerusalem hills.

After observation and examination I was classified as a paranoid schizophrenic. I spent two and a half years there and they treated me with drugs. I had so many drugs that they finally stopped having any effect on me.

Conditions in the hospital were actually quite comfortable. I had a warm bed and plenty of food. The staff did what they could to help but it was all to no avail. I was very miserable and behaved like a mentally-ill person. I was very violent and would occasionally try to commit suicide.

A psychiatric hospital is a terrible place to be, riddled with demons. There is no rest and no peace and no quiet. You just can't get any real sleep. Whenever I needed some hours of deep sleep I would break some windows or attack someone. They would then give me Valium intravenously and I could get a few hours of really deep and nightmare-free sleep. That was the best thing I could hope for in that place.

There was one psychologist there who abused his position and humiliated the patients. He had a position of power and with one pen stroke he could determine a patient's destiny for good or for ill. One day he lied about me. It made me so furious that I went into the kitchen and grabbed the first implement I saw which happened to be a fork and threw it at him with all my strength. It struck him on the head and caused a deep gash which needed stitching.

Usually in such situations they would tie me up and leave me alone for a while in a secluded ward. This time however they decided that they had had enough of me and simply discharged me from hospital, which was against all regulations.

No one wanted to take me in. My parents and friends were afraid of me. I tried returning to Eitanim but they refused to take me back. I then lived alone in the forests of the Jerusalem hills. I thought to myself: 'This is it. I have no more hope. I must commit suicide and be done with all my troubles.'

I took off my belt and tied it to a tree but then felt a real physical force preventing me from going ahead with my plan. I decided instead to starve myself to death and so started to fast. I sat there all alone in the forest and waited for death to release me from my misery.

It was rather boring just sitting there doing nothing. Not thinking much I took out the Bible I always carried in my pack and started reading it again for the first time in many years.

I read and read and whilst reading the Bible out there amongst the trees something happened to me. I was still confused from the effects of the drugs and my heart was still black with sin, but I felt as though a ray of light had penetrated right into me and shed some light into the darkness of my soul. Eight days I spent there alone in the woods and then suddenly I had inner peace. All my confused thoughts and all my internal struggles were suddenly removed and I felt a peace I had never had before.

I felt that I ought to go to Nueiba in the Sinai and look up John, a Dutch believer I had met before in Eilat. When I got to Nueiba John wasn't there as he had left for

Jerusalem. I waited for him and he returned after two days. I then joined a group of people who slept in his tent and studied the Bible with him.

In spite of the experience I had been through I was not yet completely healed. I had been freed from my drug habit but was still smoking three packs of cigarettes a day. I was still hurting inside and very bitter; it wasn't pleasant for anyone to be in my company. I couldn't forgive others—I still needed a loving hand to touch me and heal me completely. I heard about God who had performed miracles in the past and would yet act wonderfully in the future—but I needed a God who would perform a miracle in me today!

I thought that maybe the last days would be my solution. When the Messiah returned he would heal me. So I started a serious study of the end-time prophecies.

Finally I gave it all up. I couldn't take any more. I had just received some compensation for disability and decided to use the money to sail to the island of Patmos in Greece where the Apostle John had received the revelation of the last day events. I would live there in a cave and maybe I too would be granted a revelation of the time of Messiah's return.

Before leaving Eilat I sat together with John and his friend Johan in a car and we prayed. I prayed too, not out of conviction but rather to impress on the others that I was OK too. I said: 'Lord, not my will but yours be done.'

I did not really mean it, but the fact that I said it and maybe meant it in some little part changed my life. I had opened a door for God to work in me.

I went to Haifa where I bought a ferry ticket to Cyprus as the first stage of my trip to Patmos. I was placed in a four-berth cabin with three other young men. We started talking and I discovered that they were believers too. We spoke a lot about our faith and they explained that we

cannot limit God by our own finite human mind or box
him in by our own rules. God is sovereign and does what
he wants to do with mighty power. Miracles can happen
today even in our own lives.

Early in the morning we reached Limassol. I stood alone
on the deck. I wasn't a nice sight: a lonely figure with long,
dishevelled hair, an earring in one ear, a long black coat and
high boots, a typical traveller. Suddenly I heard a loud
voice say: 'Go and tell your cabin-mates that you want to
join them.'

I said: 'But they won't want me. No one ever wants me.'

Again I heard the clear and authoritative voice say: 'Go
and travel with them.'

I knew that I had to obey otherwise I would go completely mad. I went up to them and asked them if I could
join them on their way. They immediately agreed without
any hesitation and said that they intended going to a Christian Youth Centre some two hours drive from Limassol.
For some reason we kept losing our way and finally got
there after nine hours.

The next morning I sat down and talked to a staff
member for some hours. I realised that though I knew
much about God I still didn't know him personally. They
then invited me to attend a prayer meeting. During that
time of prayer one of them turned to me and said that he
felt led to lay hands on me and pray for me.

I was rather frightened at his suggestion but thought that
as I was in such a bad state I really had nothing to lose.
Who knows, it might even help me! He placed his hands on
my head and started to pray. Suddenly I saw the Messiah
with his arms outstretched to embrace me. I realised that
for six whole years I had been running away from him. He
said to me: 'I love you.' I said: 'Leave me alone to live my

own life.' He didn't give up. He turned to me again and again declaring: 'I love you.'

Finally I broke down and wept. I said: 'For many years I have tried to manage my life on my own and have finally reached the gutter. Take my life and do with me as you will but please help me!'

I felt as though a dark and heavy blanket was suddenly being lifted from me. I felt a tremendous sense of relief as though a heavy weight of many tons had been removed from me. I felt light and free and clean.

I asked if I could stay at the centre for a while and they agreed. I would work during the day and study in the evenings. I tried to imitate those around me and lead as 'good' a life as they did, but I didn't succeed.

One day as I was reading my Bible I suddenly saw myself standing underneath a waterfall of streaming light. The water of light fell on me, swept over me and washed me inside out. It purified me. Again I saw the Messiah and I joyfully ran towards him. He picked me up in his arms and embraced me. I felt I had finally returned to my father and that I was now completely healed.

All that day I sang and praised him with great joy. I thanked him for all he had done in my life and for his love to me. From that day on my life was truly changed for the better.

I spent a year in Cyprus at that Christian Youth Centre. There I learned the basis of the life of faith and God cleansed me from all the vile things that had stuck to me during the many years of darkness and sin.

I needed the discipline of regular Bible study, prayer and work that I found there. God also taught me how to make the right decisions—it wasn't easy after so many years of always making the wrong ones. I also received lots of love and support from the staff, and lots of counselling too. I desperately needed all that I could get!

After a year spent there I returned to Israel as a new and changed person. God directed me to Tel-Aviv where I worked for a while as a volunteer at the messianic centre 'Beit Immanuel'. Whilst working there I met my future wife Shlomit from Switzerland, who was also a volunteer there.

One day I decided to visit the psychiatrist who had treated me in Eitanim. He couldn't believe his eyes when he saw me sane and healthy in front of him. 'What a miracle, what a miracle!' he kept muttering. I told him that while I was drowning in deep waters he stood at the water edge and gave me good advice, but Yeshua jumped into the water and saved me from a certain death.

Later I worked as the maintenance caretaker of the centre. I was then asked to run the messianic bookshop on Ben-Yehuda Street. After that I returned to manage the hostel at Beit-Immanuel. During those busy years we got married and our two eldest boys Daniel and Yair were born.

Some time later we decided to move to Tivon in Galilee where our third boy Elad was born during the Gulf War. I found employment with a firm called Galcom which was managed by messianic believers and we joined a messianic congregation in Nazareth in which we are active today.

On my return to Israel I tried to re-establish contact with my parents. I could now forgive them and love them. My father didn't want to talk to me, he had wiped me out of his life. However gradually our relationship was renewed and slowly improved, and today we enjoy good contact with them.

The moment I believed I began to understand the world around me. Questions that had bothered me since I was a child now received satisfactory answers. Above all I now have a living relationship with my Creator. Faith isn't a legal code — it is a living relationship between man and God based on love. I don't want my behaviour to hurt God because I love him. If I inadvertently do hurt him I am quick to confess my sin and beg his forgiveness so that our relationship can be restored.

Anyone who honestly examines the Bible will see that the only one who ever fulfilled the messianic prophecies of the Tenach was Yeshua. Whoever believes in him returns to true biblical Judaism, to the real roots of our people. The way to God is clearly revealed in the Tenach and in the New Testament, and it leads through the atoning death of Yeshua the Messiah for our sins.

The sacrifice has been offered, the blood has been shed and my sins are forgiven. In his death Yeshua took my old life of sin and gave me his holy life in exchange for it.

As I look back on my years of wandering in the darkness, I thank God for saving me from slavery to drugs and from a confused mind and for giving me new life in Yeshua.

# 10

# Hadassah—Through Crisis to Faith

*I have always* loved painting. In times of crisis painting helps me give vent to my pent-up feelings, and over the years I have accumulated a large collection of my own paintings.

One day in December 1990 I decided to look through the collection and bring some order into it. Whilst I was busy doing this, I came across an old diary of mine that had somehow fallen in between the canvases. I took it out, dusted it, sat down in an armchair and started to read. It was an interesting journey back into my past. Every page brought back memories, experiences and faces. In my mind's eye I travelled back in time as my life-story unfolded before me.

My life has had its ups and downs and I have gone through much pain and frustration. It was in times of crisis that I started asking questions about life's meaning and goal.

My parents came to the land of Israel in what is called the

fifth Aliyah (wave of immigration) in 1936. Both of them came from Poland, from families that kept the Jewish traditions such as the Sabbath, the Jewish Holy Days and kashrut. Both of them rebelled against religion and tradition whilst in their early teens, like many others of their generation.

After completing only primary school, they left parents and home in order to join the Zionist-Marxist movement called 'Hashomer Hatzair'. There they were trained for their future agricultural way of life in a kibbutz in Israel.

They were the rebels, and thanks to their emigration to Israel they were the sole survivors of their respective families. All their relatives were later annihilated during the Nazi holocaust. Of my mother's family only one brother survived and he now lives in Bat-Yam.

They were willing to sacrifice their families, educational prospects and potential careers in Poland for the sake of their ideals. Their vision was to found a new society based on equality in a reborn Jewish people living in their ancient homeland, thus fulfilling both their Zionist and their Socialist dreams in the same land.

They arrived in the land of Israel during the British mandate, at the time of an Arab uprising when marauding Arab bands were attacking Jewish settlements. My parents were assigned to the small group of people that was to found the Kibbutz Nir-David in the Beit Shean valley, still a dangerous place at that time. Malaria was endemic, and Jewish settlements were harassed by Arab bands.

One of the curiosities of that time was an old Ottoman law that allowed the erection of a new settlement only if its houses could all be built during one night. The roofs had to be finished by dawn!

As a result the Jewish authorities planned a new type of village, called a 'wall and tower' settlement, that could be erected in just one night and included a defensive wall around the houses and a watch-tower. Nir-David was the first kibbutz to be built under this new system. Many similar villages were later built to the same pattern.

My parents were firmly committed to their ideals. Like many of the pioneers of the founding generation, they invested all their lives in making their dreams come true. They experienced much suffering as they drained the swamps, ploughed the fields and brought into being a new Jewish community based on hard work, equal opportunities and a communal lifestyle. These were the ingredients that enabled their kibbutz to survive, develop and flourish.

I was their eldest child, born in 1942. They had three boys after me, the last two being twins.

I grew up in the communal children's home typical of a kibbutz. By keeping the children in special homes under qualified supervision the parents were enabled to devote their time and energy to the kibbutz work, men and women sharing the workload equally.

Every child had his own bed and wardrobe—this was his only private corner where he could keep his belongings and the collections children are so fond of. Everything else was shared—the room, the meals and the studies. We were always together and learned to share and to give. I had no special problem with the system—I accepted it as a self-understood part of my life.

I remember that there were two main problems that bothered me during my childhood years. The first one was that I loved sleeping and found it extremely difficult to wake up on time for school in the morning. This problem haunted me for many years. The staff tried hard to help me—it worried them more than it worried me!

The second problem was that I did not like to eat. I had

no appetite and food simply had no attraction for me. This caused a prolonged conflict with my mother who was always concerned about my health and physical development. She was forever nagging me with that everlasting question: 'Have you had anything to eat yet? '

In 1948 whilst I was still in kindergarten the War of Independence broke out. It was the first time I had really felt afraid. Every time the sirens sounded we had to run to the shelter. One night the neighbouring kibbutz was shelled, and we had to run to the shelter at midnight and stay there till the morning. During that war, the fathers of three children in my group were killed, and it was a traumatic experience for us to face bereavement, mourning and visits to the cemetery.

At school I enjoyed the humanities but found mathematics and science rather difficult. I loved collecting things such as marbles and pictures and exchanging them with my friends.

At the age of twelve I started piano lessons, and later I also learned to play the flute. Once a week I was sent to the music centre at Kibbutz Ein Harod and I really loved it. I still play these instruments today and have a great love of classical music.

At high school I was very active on various pupils' committees. I joined the drama club and fell in love with Israeli folk dancing which became my main hobby.

I was also a member of the Hashomer-Hatzair youth movement. At that time the youth movements still had a great influence on children. We were taught to respect the values of Zionism and Socialism and to endeavour to put them into practice. We were also taught to co-exist with the Arabs in the land, believing that Jews and Arabs could peacefully live alongside each other.

In the framework of my youth movement involvement,

I was sent to be a guide to younger children in the neighbouring town of Beit-Shean, which at that time was a poor immigrant city. I taught them folk dancing at their local youth club and built a good relationship with them. We leaders from the kibbutz invited them to our village and got them involved in various activities.

I loved my father very much. He was a self-taught man, very knowledgeable in literature, history and philosophy. He was always interested in my progress at school and he used to help me with my studies and encouraged me to develop my gifts. I learned a lot from him, and owe him my drive to study more and use my gifts to the full.

My relationship with my mother was very different. She was a rather stubborn woman with narrow views. All she asked of me was that I should be clean and tidy—and that I should eat. For many years we had conflicts in these areas. We weren't close to each other and I couldn't learn from her as I could from my dad.

Whilst teaching folk dancing in Beit-Shean I got to know a young fellow called Nachman who had joined our dancing group. He was two and a half years older than me, tall, dark, very handsome and an excellent dancer. He was the seventh and youngest child of a large family originally from Iraq. His father had been murdered in Iraq and his mother had brought the children to Israel and had settled in Beit-Shean, where she worked very hard to make ends meet. Immediately on completion of primary school, Nachman had to go out and find a job so he could help support the family.

I was then seventeen years old and this was my first deep relationship with a man. I had had some childish love affairs that had petered out. I fell in love with Nachman almost at first sight and we dated each other for three years.

I was called up to the army in 1959 and after six weeks of

initial training I was allocated to the ordnance corps base in Haifa, not far from the naval base where Nachman served as a mechanic. We saw a lot of each other during that time and our relationship deepened and developed until we decided to get married.

My parents weren't at all happy with our relationship. My mother especially was very much opposed to it. The fact that Nachman was from an Oriental community and that he hadn't finished high school disturbed her. 'You deserve someone better than that,' she would say, though she didn't really know him or his character. This was my second big conflict with my mum.

My beloved father died of a heart attack at the age of fifty-one when I was nineteen. I was still in the army when I heard the bitter news. The whole family was still so much in need of him; my brothers were still so young. We now lacked his guidance and couldn't give him the joy of seeing us maturing. 'I have lost my dear dad,' I thought to myself as tears coursed down my cheeks. 'Why did this have to happen to me?' There was no answer to this question and there was no comfort for my sorrow. I heard people say 'God has given and God has taken away,' but that attitude of mind was meaningless to me.

My mother who had always been a strong and dominant character now took over the leadership of our little family, and she held on to that position until she had seen all of us safely married. She is now eighty years old and still living on the kibbutz.

Mother was now very interested in having a male figure in the family to help bring up my twelve-year-old twin brothers, so she changed her mind about us and started pushing us to get married fast. We didn't need much encouragement in that direction, so we decided to get married immediately on my release from army service.

We were married in 1961 and Nachman joined our kibbutz. My mother was now pleased to have a man at home who lent a hand with bringing up the boys. Nachman was very good to them, and both Amos and Yoram have fond memories of him.

We were very much in love. It was a young, blind and immature love. We enjoyed being together and had joint interests in folk dancing, swimming and various sports. Nachman was a very clean and tidy fellow. He was good with his hands and always helped me with the housework. In the kibbutz he was employed as a mechanic and driver for the Beit Shean-Harod co-operative. He was a good worker and was popular both with his work-mates and with our friends. After a while, even my mother came to accept and love him.

During our first years of marriage we were very happy. One year in our holidays we travelled to Europe, and I felt on cloud nine! I discovered a new world, with old cultures and new landscapes which I thoroughly enjoyed.

After four years of marriage, our daughter Sigal was born. My joy was now complete and I felt I had everything I could wish for.

Five years into marriage, however, tensions and conflicts between us appeared that had lain dormant beneath the surface during the first happy years. Nachman found it very difficult to adapt to kibbutz life. He came from a traditional home and the demonstrative secularism of the kibbutz disturbed him. He also found it difficult to accept that on the kibbutz everyone received according to their needs irrespective of their contribution. He was sure there were people who exploited the system and lived at others' expense.

Beyond our common interests, there were other areas I was deeply interested in: literature, art, music and the theatre. I couldn't share these with Nachman at all. I wanted to develop and grow in these areas, and I wanted to involve my husband in them, but Nachman had no interest whatsoever. His world seemed to me now to be very narrow and confined.

Because of his background, Nachman also felt that a woman should take care of home and children and shouldn't work outside the home. Though he had become a kibbutz member, deep down he resented the communal lifestyle, and gradually he started to apply pressure on me to leave the kibbutz.

I wouldn't even hear of it! I firmly believed that the kibbutz was the best society in the world, and I wouldn't dream of leaving it.

Nachman loved me and Sigal, but these tensions continued to grow and finally blew up. The gap between our positions widened until Nachman suggested that he should leave the kibbutz alone. If I joined him after a specified time, fine. If not, we would get a divorce.

He used to visit us once a week, and each time he came we would go over the same arguments and the hurts deepened. We loved each other and felt we belonged together. Our little girl was only two and a half years old and I was still a young woman of twenty-six. But the differences in our backgrounds and lifestyle proved to be too strong, and finally in 1968 we got a divorce. My first real love and with it all my hopes and security were now dashed to pieces.

Nachman claimed Sigal, but as I stayed on in the sheltered life of the kibbutz, the court gave custody to me. Nachman left us and Nir-David. He later married again and left for South Africa and then Australia where he still lives today.

This was a very deep and painful wound that took many

years to heal. Had I then had the experience and maturity I have today, we wouldn't have reached the divorce court.

I was devastated when Nachman left us. All the security of an ordered and safe married life, with a man at my side to help in times of crisis, was now gone as though it had never even existed. I had deep fears about how I would cope as a single parent on the kibbutz. A kibbutz is a small and closed world where exceptions are not easily tolerated. Friends who used to visit us as a couple stopped dropping in. The men were afraid of their wives' jealousy, and the women now saw in me a potential competitor. It was most unpleasant, and was one of the toughest periods of my life.

I spent some very difficult years as a divorcee on the kibbutz, years of struggle and of adaptation in which many of my basic assumptions about life were badly shaken. When asked about my future I would say that all I could see was an empty white screen on which not even one line was drawn.

On the other hand, I was still young and vivacious. I had always been a spontaneous, romantic and excitable type. I loved dressing well and enjoyed having a good time in the kibbutz disco. Men were attracted to me, and that brought me into a moral dilemma. I was brought up with high moral standards—no sex outside of marriage. I wanted a partner for life—not for one night. Some men couldn't understand that. They thought a divorced and lonely woman was fair prey. At any rate, I did overcome initial temptations and never had a relationship with any of them.

I decided that I needed to build up a new image of myself as a serious and responsible woman. This was a long drawn-out process that took several years to accomplish, but it did finally make its impact on our society.

I had now lost both my father and my husband. As a result of these losses I started searching for love and security. I went out of my way to meet new people and get acquainted with new ways and ideas.

During these years I brought up my daughter with lots of love and devotion and today she is my best friend as well as being my beloved daughter.

After the Six Day War in 1967, volunteers from abroad started arriving at the kibbutz. I used the opportunity to practise and improve my English, and spent a lot of time talking to them. They wanted to know about our communal lifestyle and about the Arab-Israeli conflict, whilst I was interested in the world they came from. These conversations widened my horizons as I heard of various lifestyles and philosophies that were so different to my own.

One of my brothers fell in love with a Swiss volunteer. They later got married and lived in Nir-David.

In 1972 a young Swiss volunteer named Roland arrived at Nir-David. He was a good friend of my sister-in-law and so I got to meet him too. Roland arrived as a traveller in faded clothes and long hair and beard. In Switzerland he had rebelled against his bourgeois parents and against the establishment. He left home and started travelling around the world searching for his identity.

I had many deep conversations with Roland on the meaning of life, philosophy and kibbutz principles. We had both arrived at a watershed in our lives where we were searching for meaning and for truth in this world.

Our relationship grew and deepened through this contact and the exchange of views. After five years of acquaintance, we moved in together. Roland then decided to acquire Israeli citizenship, served in the army and became a kibbutz member.

Once again I had the security of living with a man who loved me. We had some problems, mainly because Roland was jealous of my deep relationship with Sigal, but we overcame this and we had many common interests. My life was once again settled and ordered and it looked as though I didn't lack a thing.

However, just at that time in the early seventies when my life was on an even keel, I began to feel an emptiness within me that I was unable to fill. Once, going out for a walk with a friend I asked her: 'What is wrong with me? Do you also feel this way? I long for something, but I don't know what it is I long for. I seem to have everything, yet something is lacking!'

This feeling would come over me especially when I was outside in the country enjoying the beauty of nature, or when I was admiring a beautiful work of art or listening to good music. There was a void within me, and I started to search for something to fill it.

I shared these feelings with Roland, and he told me about his own search for meaning in his church in Switzerland. He had left the Protestant Church deeply disappointed by the hypocrisy he saw there. The nice people you met on Sunday seemed so different during the week. That society seemed distorted and sick and he searched for a better world. He had also tried drugs during his travels but they didn't meet his deep spiritual needs.

We decided to search together. We read about parapsychology, we took a course in transcendental meditation and performed yoga exercises. I had many questions and was desperately searching for answers: Who am I? Why am I in this world? Where am I going? What is the meaning of my life?

In 1978 Michael, an old friend of Roland who had studied Hebrew with him on the kibbutz years before, paid us a visit. He was reading a book called *The Late Great Planet Earth* which he found very interesting. It dealt with biblical prophecies being fulfilled today in Israel and in the modern world. Michael loaned us the book, and he later brought me a Hebrew translation of it.

One day I sat alone outside on the green lawn and finished reading through the book. I was gripped by it. On the last page it said: 'If you want, you can accept Yeshua into your life. All alone and in your own words.'

The book had really impressed me. In the Hashomer-Hatzair kibbutzim the philosophy of life is atheistic. There is some supreme force out there, which you may call God—that is the most that they are willing to concede. But this force is a mechanistic and random force, it is not the God of the Bible.

In the book I had just read I met a different God, a God who ruled history and was also interested in individuals, a personal God who seeks for a personal relationship with his creatures. Out there alone on the grass I did exactly as had been suggested. I said to him: 'Maybe you are what I am searching for, what I lack, what I am longing for. I receive you into my life.'

I did not know much about Yeshua. In history class they had always connected Yeshua to the Christianity that had persecuted the Jews and had even burnt them at the stake during the period of the Inquisition. I had never grasped that Yeshua was a Jew who was born in Galilee, or that he had claimed to be the Messiah of Israel.

When we graduated from high school, we were all presented with a copy of the Tenach. For many years my copy had lain unused on a shelf. I now got it down, dusted it, and began to read it.

We had studied the prophets at school—Isaiah, Jeremiah, Amos and others—but we had never connected them to the future of Israel or to the Messiah. I now read them again as I compared the claims of the book I had read with the Tenach. I came to realise that all the book said was actually based on the Scriptures.

I was working in the Ulpan at that time, and I remembered that the Scottish Church in Tiberias had recently sent our Ulpan some free copies of the Hebrew Bible which included the New Testament. I opened one such book and started to read through the New Testament. Suddenly I thought to myself: 'How could I have been so blind for so many years?' I saw that Yeshua had fulfilled many of the prophecies of the Tenach. I now felt a great hunger to know more about him. Every evening after work I would sit down and read the Tenach and the Brit Hadashah. I read right through the Gospels, and all I read had the ring of truth in it and seemed very reasonable.

Some days later, our Ulpan went on a trip to Jerusalem. On the way back I spoke to one of our students, Tal, who with his wife Adi had recently made Aliyah to Israel from the USA and was now learning Hebrew.

We spoke about Jerusalem and the Western Wall. We spoke about the city's spiritual meaning to our people and about the question of faith in God. As our conversation progressed, I told Tal about the book *The Late Great Planet Earth* that I had recently read, and how it had led me to read the Tenach and the New Testament. I told him that I now believed in God and in Yeshua as the Messiah. I was pleasantly surprised to discover that Tal too believed in Yeshua. He had come to faith during his student years in a university in the States. When we got back to Nir-David we lingered for a long time near the bus, in the dark and in the cold winter weather, engrossed in conversation about our mutual faith.

That same week Tal gave me several other books in Hebrew that dealt with the messianic faith. I read all of them and continued reading the Bible hungrily. I now felt a deep peace and a wonderful joy. As I looked through my diary the other day, I found that I had written these words at that time: 'Now I know! Now the void within me is being filled!'

Of course I shared my discovery with Roland, and he too read the book and seemed to be convinced. Later on we heard of messianic Jews living in the nearby town of Afula. We visited them and started attending the small congregation there. We were overjoyed to meet brothers and sisters in the faith. At that same time we also experienced God blessing us in a special way. I was given a job as an art and creativity teacher in the kibbutz school, something I had always aspired to be, and Roland received permission to develop riding stables in the kibbutz, something he had been asking for over several years.

Some years later, when Sigal was sixteen years old, she too came to faith. We now enjoyed a wonderful spiritual unity in our family. Roland's relationship to Sigal improved greatly. I felt that I finally had a real partner for life with whom I could share in all areas—literature, art, my love of nature, and now also my faith in Yeshua.

These were the best years of my life. We walked along this new road together. In the evenings, after the day's work was done, we would sit at home and sing songs of praise. Roland and Sigal played their guitars, and I joined on the flute. Visitors would happily join in the singing. It was a wonderful time of harmony and full partnership that lasted for six years.

The news about our new-found faith quickly spread around the kibbutz and there was a lot of gossip. Most people thought that we had joined some weird sect. As a result we were one day called to the kibbutz secretariat for an interview during which they asked us to stop visiting the congregation in Afula.

We explained that we had not changed our religion and that we had not joined a sect. We also asked them whether our behaviour and contribution to the kibbutz had deteriorated in any way. Of course, the opposite was true, and they left it at that and have since left us alone.

We didn't force our views on anyone, but many people asked us questions and we could explain things to them. Kibbutzniks don't lack for any material things; they don't feel that they need the good news of faith in Yeshua. It is only people who have gone through a crisis who start searching and are willing to open their hearts.

Most of the reactions to our faith were negative. My brothers thought that I had gone crazy. Close friends turned their backs on us, but others showed an interest and we had some very good conversations with them.

In 1986, after fifteen years of living together, Roland and I felt that it was right to have an official wedding. We went to Switzerland, to Roland's home town where we had a civil ceremony and then a service in a congregation of some two hundred believers who accepted us with open arms. Roland's brother and sister-in-law also came to faith around that time and we spent some wonderful weeks with them in Switzerland.

Some years earlier, in 1978, my brother and his Swiss wife had left the kibbutz and gone to Switzerland. They had a pony they really liked, and they asked us to look after it for a year or two until they were settled and could get it shipped over.

Whilst caring for this pony, Roland fell in love with horses. He started riding and learning all he could about horses. He read all the books he could lay his hands on and got completely engrossed in the subject in addition to his regular work in the cotton branch of the kibbutz.

As he got more and more involved with horses, the hobby became his real vision and mission in life. He realised that horses could be used to make kibbutz life more appealing to the younger generation who were tempted to leave and start a new life in the cities. Roland started giving riding lessons to children and youngsters on the kibbutz, and after ten years of involvement in this hobby he finally received official permission from the kibbutz authorities to open a riding school and further develop the stables.

From the moment he fell in love with horses, he gave this hobby all he had. Sigal and I got involved with it too. At forty, I was the first woman on the kibbutz to ride a horse. We would go on riding treks together and I helped to clean the stables and with other odd jobs.

I felt that the more Roland got involved with this new passion of his, the more his spiritual life deteriorated. It was a slow but steady decline. He stopped attending the services at the congregation, his interest in spiritual matters waned and our partnership in the faith came to an end.

He had a riding pupil who had started taking lessons when she was only twelve years old. Later she started working in the stables and became a riding instructor. The relationship between them developed until in March of 1990 Roland left me and Sigal and went to live with this young girl who was now eighteen years old and had just started her army service.

At this sad stage of my life, when I was up against a new crisis and was feeling weak and miserable, I found comfort and encouragement in my faith in Yeshua. This time I did not feel lonely, Yeshua was so near to me that I sometimes felt as though he had laid his hand on my shoulder to strengthen me.

At first I felt a lot of anger and bitterness welling up within me, but I prayed that God would not allow these feelings to poison my soul and spirit. I also prayed that God would forgive Roland and help me to forgive him too.

God answered my prayers and restored to me the joy I had before. He strengthened me too, so that I now can meet Roland, shake his hand and talk to him without any feelings of jealousy or bitterness. Only God's love could effect this great change in me.

'Rather, as servants of God we commend ourselves in every way: in great endurance; in troubles, hardships and distresses...sorrowful, yet always rejoicing; poor, yet making many rich; having nothing, and yet possessing everything.' These verses from the New Testament (2 Corinthians chapter 6, verses 4 and 10) faithfully reflect my feelings today as I serve God in the community I was born into here in Nir-David.

The world is in chaos. Personal ambition drives most people forward and causes them to sell their birthright. We worship outward beauty and ignore the inner man. Scientific and technological achievements arm the world with the most destructive weapons imaginable. News of wars, famine and disaster outweigh news about peace and good will between nations. Morals have broken down and 'every man does that which seems right in his own eyes'. In a world such as this man needs a hiding place, a shelter where he can find peace and healing. We are desperately in need of faith, hope and love. Only Yeshua, the Jew, the carpenter's son from Nazareth, can give us all of these.

For two thousand years we have been searching for him, for the promised Messiah, and on him, the solid rock, I have rebuilt the shambles of my broken life. Yeshua guides me day by day, comforts me in my pain and channels his love to others through me. He has worked a real miracle in my life.

On looking back over my life, the last eleven years since

I came to believe in Yeshua look like an exciting adventure in spite of the difficulties. God taught me many things about myself, and I have learnt to look at my past without anger or bitterness and at the same time look forward with hope to the future. God also taught me that as a believer who has been born again I need to change and to grow in my faith.

I am sure that my sins are forgiven through the sacrifice of the Messiah. Every now and then he sheds light on other sins in my life that I hadn't noticed before, new areas of my life that he needs to purify and change. This is a daily challenge and struggle, and I must daily choose between my own wishes and feelings and focussing on Yeshua and his will for my life.

With the aid of a Bible study course by extension from the Caspari Institute in Jerusalem, I could study the Scriptures and get to know them better. I also read many messianic books that helped me to better understand the messianic faith. Reading, prayer, fellowship at the congregation and at conferences have filled my life with new meaning.

I realised that it wasn't enough to get to know Yeshua the day I first believed. I had to walk with him all along the road and live according to his will in order to reflect something of his light to others. As people saw the way I overcame these crises in my life they would approach me and ask me for my secret.

Today I am content with my lot. I am happy in my work with the school children. I invest a lot in them and see good results plus developing good relationships with them. I have good fellowship with many brothers and sisters in the faith, and Sigal my daughter is still with me.

In spite of the suffering and turmoil I've been through, I

can testify that through my faith in Yeshua God has strengthened and encouraged me. My ambition now is to serve him faithfully here in the kibbutz, and my hope is that others will recognise God's plan for Israel and for the world as revealed in the Bible and that they will accept Yeshua as the promised Messiah of our people.

# Postscript

*I hope you have* enjoyed this collection of true life stories. Maybe you could identify with some of the characters or events in the book. Maybe you too are searching for a way out of life's bewildering maze.

Through the circumstances of life and through crises and difficulties God gradually led these people towards the great discovery: they all found Yeshua the Messiah as the missing link in their lives and in the history of the Jewish nation.

You too can find him. Yeshua is the Messiah promised by the prophets in the Tenach. He is the sacrifice that God provided in order to forgive your sins and to bring you into a living relationship with himself.

All alone, in the privacy of your home or any other place you may be in, you too can turn directly to God and simply say to him: 'I receive Yeshua into my life, I need him, and I thank you that through him you have solved my problem of sin and of alienation from yourself.'

God does not enter our lives by force. He prepares the

circumstances and he knocks on the door of our heart. Everyone ought to respond positively to God's initiative. If you will do this, you will receive a new life just as these people did.

God has promised to receive everyone who comes to him in this simple way. He will receive you as you are and will then change you from within. He will forgive your sins, cleanse you and give you the power to live in joy and peace in this world.

Trust God—open your life to him—and go on your way with Yeshua the Messiah!

If you have put your trust in him, you must now develop your faith and your spiritual life:

1. Read the Bible regularly—it is your spiritual food.

2. Pray to God through the Messiah in simple and spontaneous words. This is your personal link to God. Pour out your heart to him, silence your heart before him and listen to his voice.

3. Find friends with similar beliefs. There are many scattered all over the world as individuals and in congregations. You need their encouragement and support.

4. Talk about your faith to others—don't be ashamed of it.

If you would like further advice and help in knowing Yeshua and following him, please write to:

> David Zeidan
> PO Box 27
> Carlisle
> Cumbria
> CA1 2HG
> England

# Glossary

*Aliyah*—Immigration to Israel; literally means 'going up'.

*Ashkenazi*—Belonging to one of the many Jewish communities with their roots in medieval France and Germany and who later spread to Eastern Europe and other centres.

*Bar Mitzvah*—Confirmation for a boy on his thirteenth birthday when he comes of age and is considered an adult man for religious purposes.

*Bnei Akivah*—Youth movement run by the National-Religious party.

*Brit Hadashah*—New Testament; literally means 'New Covenant'.

*Cheder*—Traditional orthodox elementary school for boys (often starting when they were three years old) where they learnt the alphabet, the Pentateuch and the basics of Judaism.

*Couscous*—Popular traditional North African dish of steamed wheat cereal with meat and vegetables.

*Diaspora*—The Jewish exile; the dispersion; used to describe the Jews scattered all over the world and the countries they live in.

*Gefillte fish*—Traditional Jewish dish of Eastern European origin eaten on the Sabbath and other religious holidays.

*Hanukkah*—The feast of lights, commemorating the rededication of the Temple by the Maccabees.

*Hashomer Hatzair*—The youth movement connected to the Marxist-Zionist Mapam political party.

*Hassidim*—Influential mystical movement in orthodox Judaism; started in 17th century Eastern Europe.

*Irgun*—Nationalist Zionist political-military movement that developed in opposition to the mainline socialist parties and advocated extreme action against the British and the Arabs in pre-independence Israel. Menachem Begin was the leader of the Irgun.

*Kashrut*—The complex body of orthodox Jewish dietary laws.

*Kibbutz*—Communal village where all land and production means are communally owned.

*Kippah*—Skull-cap worn by observant Jews at all times, except in sleep.

*Mapai*—The Workers' Party of Israel; main political party (socialist) in pre-independence Israel, and the first two decades following independence. Ben-Gurion was the leader of Mapai.

*Mapam*—The United Workers' Party; left-wing Zionist-Marxist political party that established many kibbutzim and has a strong youth movement called Hashomer-Hatzair.

*Mashiach*—Messiah, the anointed one, the Christ.

*Matzot*—Unleavened bread used at Passover.

*Mezuzot*—Tiny boxes containing a hand-written parchment inscribed with the Shema (Hear O Israel) and excerpts from the Ten Commandments. The Mezuzot are fastened to every door-post of a Jewish dwelling in obedience to the command 'You shall write them on your door-posts.'

*Minyan*—Quorum of ten males needed for any orthodox religious service, especially prayer.

*Mitzvot*—Commandments.

*Moshav*—Co-operative village, where each family owns its own house and land, but the production and sale is done communally.

*Penitent*—A secular Jew who turns back to orthodox Judaism and becomes religious.

*Pessach*—The Passover feast.

*Purim*—The feast commemorating the deliverance of the Jews in the Persian Empire from annihilation at the hand of Haman. Queen Esther intervened to save her people.

*Rashi*—Authoritative medieval Rabbi and his commentary on the Torah.

*Sabbath*—The seventh day of the week, the day of rest.

*Sabra*—Someone born in Israel.

*Sephardic*—belonging to one of the many Jewish communities (mainly Mediterranean and Middle East) that originated with the expulsion of all Jews from Spain in 1492.

*Tallit*—Prayer shawl worn over the outer garments for morning prayers.

*Targum of Onkelos* - Ancient translation of Pentateuch into Aramaic.

*Tefillin*—Small box containing parchment with verses of Scripture bound to forehead and left arm with leather straps in daily ritual prompted by the commandment: 'Tie them as symbols on your hands and bind them on your foreheads.'

*Tenach*—Acronym for the Old Testament, meaning Torah (Pentateuch), Nevi'im (Prophets) and Ktuvim (writings).

*Ulpan*—Special language school for teaching Hebrew to new immigrants. Ulpanim are usually organised and run by public bodies such as municipalities. Many kibbutzim operate Ulpanim.

*War of Independence*—May 1948 to July 1949.

*War, Six Day*—June 1967.

*War, Yom Kippur*—October 1973.

*War, Lebanon*—June 1982.

*Yad Leachim*—Fanatical orthodox organisation devoted to fighting missionary activities.

*Yeshiva*—A religious Jewish school in which the oral law is the main subject.

*Yeshu*—Garbled Greek form of the name Jesus; derogatory name given to the Messiah by the rabbis, acronym of 'may his name and memory be blotted out'.

*Yeshua*—The Hebrew name given to the Messiah and meaning 'God saves'.

*Youth Aliyah*—Zionist organisation involved in the absorption of children and young immigrants into Israeli society.

*Zionism*—The political movement which has as its goal the regathering of the Jewish people from their exile back into the land of Israel, and the establishment of a viable and independent Jewish state there.